Storied Dishes

Storied Dishes

What Our Family Recipes Tell Us About Who We Are and Where We've Been

Linda Murray Berzok, Editor

PRAEGER

AN IMPRINT OF ABC-CLIO, LLC
Santa Barbara, California • Denver, Colorado • Oxford, England

Library of Congress Cataloging-in-Publication Data

Storied dishes : what our family recipes tell us about who we are and where we've been / Linda Murray Berzok, editor.
    p. cm.
    Includes bibliographical references and index.
    ISBN 978-0-313-38167-6 (hard copy : alk. paper)—ISBN 978-0-313-38168-3 (ebook) 1. International cooking. 2. Cooking, American. 3. Food habits—United States. 4. Families—United States. 5. Multiculturalism—United States. 6. United States—Social life and customs. I. Berzok, Linda Murray.
    TX725.A1S67   2011
    641.5973—dc22   2010034881

ISBN: 978-0-313-38167-6
EISBN: 978-0-313-38168-3

14   13   12   11   3   4   5

This book is also available on the World Wide Web as an eBook.
Visit www.abc-clio.com for details.

Praeger
An Imprint of ABC-CLIO, LLC

ABC-CLIO, LLC
130 Cremona Drive, P.O. Box 1911
Santa Barbara, California 93116-1911

This book is printed on acid-free paper ∞

Manufactured in the United States of America

The publisher has done its best to make sure the instructions and/or recipes in this book are correct. However, users should apply judgment and experience when preparing recipes, especially parents and teachers working with young people. The publisher accepts no responsibility for the outcome of any recipe included in this volume

To Auntie M—
For all she gave us

Chief of our aunts—not only I,
But all your dozen of nurslings cry—
What did the other children do?
And what were childhood, wanting you?[1]

Contents

Acknowledgments

First and foremost, I want to thank my contributors without whom there would be no book. I am fortunate to count many as personal friends, others as colleagues. My call for submissions brought responses from the Association for the Study of Food and Society (ASFS) ListServ, the Culinary Historians of New York and the Inkberry writing collective in North Adams, Massachusetts. Other contributors came through multiple sources. And then there were those who passed my posting along to women ideally suited to the book. My deepest gratitude goes to all these women who took a chance on this project and shared their memories with me.

One contributor deserves special mention: Little did I know when I walked into a memoir writing workshop in Williamstown, Massachusetts, that the facilitator Ellen Perry Berkeley, editor of *At Grandmother's Table,* would become my primary mentor and champion. Without her unflagging encouragement, I would never have persevered.

On the publishing side, I thank my Praeger editor, Emily Birch, who edited the manuscript into a far better book. Thanks also to my original editor, Tisha Hooks, who came up with the subtitle and made astute suggestions for overall organization.

As always, my life partner and husband, Bob, encourages me, reads endless drafts, puts up with my moaning and need for space to work, and is always on call to solve computer crises, many of which I generate myself. He is the best!

Introduction

MY MOTHER'S RECIPES

What woman doesn't treasure a family recipe? Even with the proliferation of online recipe sites, the *Food Network* and glossy chef cookbooks, we return time and again to those tattered index cards. Is there some umbilical force pulling us back?

When my mother died, I unearthed her top secret recipes in a kitchen cupboard, boxes crammed with handwritten, yellowing relics, literally hundreds. Each was heavily annotated in different colored inks representing different years, noting how she would improve the dish next time. My mother never met a recipe she liked, at least not at first.

For two years, these boxes sat in the nether reaches of our basement, gathering dust and mold. Then one summer day, I pulled them out to do some matrilineal excavation. I lay back on the couch and read each and every card. I laughed and I cried. I could hear my mother's voice and those of my aunts, grandmother, neighbors, and friends. Here was my grandmother's Swedish meatballs recipe, relegated by my mother to a cocktail party hors d'oeuvre rather than front and center on a traditional smorgasbord. I found my beloved Aunt Gertrude's kedgeree, a British-inspired dish of rice, cream, hard-boiled egg, and lobster—a hoity-toity combo. The eldest of my aunts, she died tragically of a brain tumor at 64. I smiled when I came across a confection my mother dubbed "Esposito Frosting," a wonderful fluffy chocolate made by the mother of my best high school friend, Rita Esposito. Spread on a white cake and refrigerated overnight, it metamorphosed into a fudge-like wonder, just the way I liked it.

My mother's collection was a combination of diary, family Bible and social notes. She recorded menus for every occasion—Thanksgiving, Memorial Day, Fourth of July, birthdays, my home wedding reception, my father's retirement party, my brother's return from naval duty in Guam. She liberally penned critiques of restaurant meals ("Salad at Club—Red cabbage, slivered cheese, croutons, romaine lettuce, carrots, garlicky"), dinners at friends' homes, and even her own entertaining. About a 1972 barbecue, she wrote, "Maybe instead of creamed carrots, just buttered. Everyone seems to be dieting." *Just buttered? Sounds pretty fattening to me.* For a holiday cocktail party, she noted having invited guests from 5 to 7: "Next time just say at 5," she amended. *Sounds like she gave up on setting a closing time.* About a 1985 dinner party where she served Armenian *Dolmar,* a dish of stuffed tomatoes, cabbage, and cucumbers, she noted, "Didn't seem to go over well." Elsewhere she concluded that this peasant stew was "just an average dish," and it was retired from her entertaining repertoire.

The only contributions from me came from the years after I had settled in New York. Tellingly, they all were all from the *New York Times* and *Gourmet,* the height of big-city culinary sophistication, or so I believed at the time. On my Chicken in Champagne Sauce card, she wrote "Takes long." She dismissed a *New York Times* Christmas plum pudding with "Don't make. V. Expensive—Lots of wk.!" On Down-Under Apple Pie from the February 1968 *Gourmet,* she wrote "not as good as regular. So-o much work. Juice was stringy." *Stringy juice?*

Some women leave diaries. My mother left recipes. For a long time, women's studies scholars have observed that women of my mother's generation didn't write about their daily lives in traditional formats. Instead, they kept journals, sent letters, commemorated in quilts and needlework. But I could find no other examples of using a recipe collection in this way. Yet, here was the story of my mother's life—growing up as the daughter of Swedish immigrants, living through the difficult years of the Great Depression and World War II (she operated a drill press while my grandmother took care of me), and emerging as a suburban housewife and schoolteacher in the late 1940s.

I had always regarded my mother's cooking as typical hum-drum 1950s—Jell-O molds, Spanish rice, pork chops and applesauce, creamed chipped beef on toast—but the collection also revealed a later adventurous departure. In the '70s, during the heart of the ethnic cooking trend, she took a course in Chinese cuisine and even invested in a wok and dumpling steamer! At a dinner party in November 1981, she recorded having made

Chinese Shrimp Puffs and Sweet and Sour Pork. Even more remarkable, for Thanksgiving 1980, that most traditional, iconic American holiday, my mother served the extended family of aunts, uncles and cousins appetizers of homemade egg rolls and what she called "Chinese crackers!" Following this offbeat first course, the meal proceeded along conventional lines of turkey, stuffing, cranberry sauce, and pumpkin pie.

Reading my mother's recipe collection, I learned not only about her life and times but also about what had shaped me and my early interest in food. I spent a lot of time in her kitchen, the nerve center of our family.

As is the custom in many Scandinavian homes, our household was plunged into a frenzy of high-volume cookie production for Christmas, a practice my mother got underway as early as August when she began baking and freezing. Every year she carefully recorded how many cookies she had made and even broke them out by variety. In 1982, for example, she baked 941 (most intended as gifts) including classic Swedish ruffled *spritz* and rounds of spicy *pepparkakor.* She also turned out Cherry Winks, with candied cherries and nuts, Toll House cookies and Hoernchens, cut-out sugar cookies, iced and decorated with colored sugars and silver dragees. In 1983, she topped out at a whopping 1,350 cookies!

Always a reactionary, I swore off baking cookies for a long time after I left home (too fussy, time-demanding and trivial). But today, every year as Christmas rolls around, I seem to fall under a spell, and, find myself inexplicably drawn to making these confections, convinced that it just isn't Christmas without them.

I use my memories prompted by reading my mother's recipe collection to measure who I am and where I've been.

My Mother's Swedish *Spritz* Cookies

Makes several dozen

2 c. (4 sticks) sweet butter, softened
1 c. sugar
2 egg yolks, slightly beaten
2 t. vanilla
4 c. all-purpose flour

1. Preheat oven to 350°F.
2. Using electric mixer, cream together butter and sugar. Add egg yolks and beat again. Add vanilla and beat. Stir in flour in gradual amounts. Chill for one hour.

3. Fit cookie press with star-shaped design and fill tube with dough. Press dough through into long ropes. Cut ropes into two-inch segments and shape each one into a closed circle. Place on cookie sheets two inches apart.
4. Bake 12 to 15 minutes until golden. Let cool on sheets for 10 minutes, then remove with spatula to dish towels on wire racks. Store in plastic containers for a few days or freeze for later use.

Spinning the Tales

In our mothers' kitchens, we don't simply combine eggs, flour, and milk. We also hear tales, and participate in an oral ritual. Otherwise, recipes would be little more than a list of ingredients. But when we wrap them in narratives, they are magically transformed.

Remember that chocolate fudge cake Mother used to make on holidays? The one with two chocolate whipped cream fillings? And the time Aunt Lillian sliced it with such a vengeance that the filling squished out all over the tablecloth? You know why she slammed that knife down so hard. She was bloody furious that cousin Elise had run off and secretly married. Now thereby hangs a tale. And one not likely to be forgotten.

In *Storied Dishes*, I've gathered compelling scripts from women from various walks of life and ethnic backgrounds, each telling the story behind one special recipe. These women come from a potpourri of cultures— Armenian, Turkish, Chinese, Mexican, American Indian, Cuban, African American, American Southern, Midwestern, hardscrabble Texan, and New Orleanian, to name just a few. This makes for a rich multicultural stew with both similarities and differences. I was struck by how often women mentioned grandmothers, the *ur*-female in their lives. Perhaps the distance of one generation removed gave a more embracing perspective. Also frequently appearing were stories in which grieving figured, since there is such a universal, cross-cultural custom of nourishing the bereaved. Distinctive too, were narratives in which attempts to replicate a classic dish from childhood proved frustrating and disappointing, not living up to the original. In these scripts, the writers struggle with the bittersweet recognition that it may not be possible to re-create beloved foods. Either memory deceives or the restoration can simply never live up to the highly-colored recollection that is an integral part of past circumstances and people.

There were also some striking cultural differences—the preference for intense sweetness in a Latin American dessert, the use of a tandoor oven for an Indian dish, chiles in Mexican *chilaquiles* and eating hard times food like lamb's fry and tongue. Each group has its own customs, festivals, and traditions. Some narratives contain political statements specific to particular ethnicities—the tale of an American Indian grandmother's garden is also a plea for a return to healthy indigenous diets rather than high-fat, Western fast food. The scripts set in Cuba underscore the sad unavailability of key ingredients, the consequence of economic constraints. Those women whose stories evolve from war-torn cultures have a special poignancy of suffering and, in some cases, genocide. A New Orleans woman remembers the devastation of Hurricane Katrina and lost family recipes.

I begin *Storied Dishes* with the past—where we've been. The first chapter, Our Foremothers, is devoted to our first role models—mothers, grandmothers, even great-grandmothers. In these narratives, the memory of this woman is central. In Chapter 2, Lost Times and Places, I look at the ability of particular storied dishes to conjure up entire lost worlds, locations we can only revisit in our memories. Chapter 3, Restoring Balance, concerns those times in our lives when things are out of joint. Here, the tales hold keys to setting things right again. So often, food has redemptive power.

Beginning in Chapter 4, Life Lessons, I turn to the present—who we are. These scripts talk about what storied dishes impart, not only about the culinary but also about life in general. Next, in Chapter 5, Bonding Together, the narratives concern the adhesive quality of special dishes to strengthen family ties and friendships, memorialize women who have passed, and keep our personal histories alive. As we grow and shape our individual identities in Chapter 6, Coming into Our Own, our storied dishes contain new scripts of independence and standing on our own. Using treasured family recipes as a point of departure, we fashion our own innovations, spin our tales with new outcomes, tweaking here, tinkering there, until the recipe and story become uniquely ours.

Family recipes offer us a glimpse into our pasts—a way to understand who we are by exploring who we were. No wonder they hold such a special place in our hearts and minds. They serve up real connection and history no matter how far we've traveled since we first tasted these dishes.

In *Storied Dishes,* you'll find a community of women with no temporal, geographic, cultural, or social boundaries, a network bound together by the powerful glue of sharing scripts grounded in food. This dynamic process is a way of bringing families, friends, and generations together in a never-ending circle.

1

Our Foremothers

For me to remember a recipe is to remember the woman it came from, how it was passed on to her, and where I can situate myself within my culinary female family.[1]

—Marion Bishop, *Recipes for Reading*

Many of our storied dishes honor those women who have come before—mothers, grandmothers, even great-grandmothers. We long to experience again the closeness, warmth, and love of their kitchens. A favorite cake, a memorable bread pudding, or a treasured hors d'oeuvre can bring to life these special women. If their precious recipes cannot be located or re-created, we feel a sense of loss. Not all our remembrances of these pivotal women are warm and fuzzy. Occasionally, they stir up disturbing memories that we would prefer to relegate to the past. No matter how we perceive our foremothers, reminiscences take us back to our roots and mark where we've been, an important part of our identities.

LOST RECIPES

Joy Santlofer

One night, I awoke in a panic. I was sure my late mother's cookbook, the 1949 edition of *The Settlement Cook Book: The Way to a Man's Heart,* had been lost. For 20 years, it had resided on the kitchen shelf in her Florida retirement home, but I could not recall what had become of it after she died seven years earlier.

I don't remember ever seeing my mother use the cookbook, or any other recipe for that matter. She was a skillful intuitive cook who continually re-styled dishes until they reached her standard of perfection. After a trip to Spain, for example, she tried hundreds of variations of gazpacho (an unheard of delicacy in suburban New Jersey in the mid '60s) until she felt she had approximated the original.

The totemic placement of *The Settlement Cook Book*, however, signaled its special meaning to her. Suddenly, desperately, I wanted to have it with me. I thought it would unlock some key to my mother's life, or at least her cooking skills. Maybe it would contain a recipe that would recreate the enveloping warmth of childhood. In my mind, the cookbook became a treasured family heirloom, similar to the painting of an ancestor who announced: *This is my past and this is part of who I am.*

After a sleepless night, I called my sister who quickly reassured me that the book was safely in her basement. I breathed a sigh of relief. She promised to mail the book to me along with a surprise.

A few days later, when I opened the package, I was startled to find that the cherished cookbook had been barely touched; only one beef stew recipe was stained, and the margins contained no notations. What was its significance? Had she received it as a gift while a young wife and mother, but quickly found that her cooking skills exceeded its instructions?

A parent's life is often a mystery to children. To fill in the empty space, I created a story to suit my needs. I decided that the cookbook was saved because it was a present from her mother, doubling its keepsake value for me.

The surprise, however, was much more interesting: a small yellow spiral notebook with RECIPES (underlined twice) written on the front. Inside were 18 entries in my mother's distinctive and somewhat illegible hand. I was thrilled to find that they included her signature dish Shrimp Marinate, the family's favorite. Originally, she made it only for company, one of which featured a visit from my husband-to-be, Jonny. He was wild about those shrimp. His enthusiasm encouraged my mother to make them more frequently, even for ordinary family dinners. We couldn't help teasing my father, who also loved the dish, that he did not rate such treatment. The dish quickly became known as "Jonny's Shrimp."

I gathered the ingredients and set about making my first—and only—batch. The results were not even close to my mother's. Maybe I didn't marinate the shrimp long enough, or they were not as fresh as hers. More likely, my mother had so altered the formula over time without recording changes that it had evolved into a totally different dish. My aunt once jokingly complained that whenever she made one of my mother's recipes, it never turned out the same.

I'm sorry I never watched my mother prepare the shrimp to learn her tricks, or asked the significance of that mysterious, unused book on her shelf. Even so, the volume packs powerful magic. A glance conjures up the taste memories of my mother's wonderful meals, transporting me to her kitchen, setting off a chain of memories of family meals, all remembered in the rosy glow of the past, re-constructed to fit my needs. The notebook gives me hope that I too may one day be able to reproduce Jonny's Shrimp. My husband would certainly be grateful!

Jonny's Shrimp

This can be used as an appetizer, salad, or summer supper. When used as an hors d'oeuvre, which is the way we ate it, the shrimp will serve at least 10. Since Jonny doesn't like vinegar, my mother substituted lemon juice for him. Either will do.

¼ c. olive oil
2 t. lemon juice
1 small onion, minced
½ c. parsley, minced
1 clove garlic, minced
2 t. horseradish
¾ t. salt
1 ½ lbs. peeled, cooked, medium shrimp

1. Place shrimp in medium bowl. In small bowl, combine first seven ingredients. Then pour over shrimp. Cover with plastic wrap and marinate overnight.
2. Arrange shrimp in large glass bowl with serving spoon and surround with small plates and forks and a plate of plain crackers. My mother set it out on the coffee table (the pink shrimp and bright green parsley are very attractive) during cocktails, before dinner. People served themselves.

BREAD OF LOVE

Sian Supski

My grandmother's hands held memories: memories of heat, memories of texture, and memories of love. It was because her hands held these that many of her recipes were not written down; she baked from memory.

As I became older, I have realized that much of my childhood is bound up with my grandmother and memories of her cooking. She loved to cook for us; I believe that she cooked as an expression of love. As her deafness worsened, the more she communicated her caring through food. As she began to experience more and more through sight, smell, and touch, she let me share in the culinary knowledge held in her hands.

Every Saturday morning, my grandmother baked bread in her kitchen in the small country town of Busselton, southwest of Perth, Australia. My grandfather would get up early to light the wood stove. It had a thermostat that read "Cool," "Moderate" and "Hot," but like so many women of her generation, she could tell the temperature simply by placing her hand inside.

When I remember my grandmother, it is hard to separate my memory of her from my memory of the kitchen where she spent so much of her later life. It was a typical 1950's kitchen with apple green cupboards and pearlescent black doorknobs. She had a long bench with a display area above it. I would sit on the bench or a stool and watch her measure flour from its calico bag, mix sugar and compressed (fresh) yeast—which had a distinctively pungent smell, and was the part I disliked most. I loathed the smell so much that when we went to buy it (in the mid-1970s it was still possible to buy fresh yeast), I would conveniently disappear so I didn't have to retrieve it from the cold storage. I didn't like the sticky texture felt through the paper wrapping, and I could never seem to get the smell off my hands for days.

I watched my grandmother mix flour, yeast, and water to make dough and knead it. Her hands picked up the dough and molded it, the heel of her palm massaged it; I never realized until I was much older how much strength she had in her arms. Eventually, her fingers knew when the dough was kneaded enough. It was important not to over-knead or the bread wouldn't achieve the right soft, fluffy texture. She placed the dough in her favorite large, green Tupperware bowl, marked it with a cross to keep it from rising too rapidly, and covered it with a linen tea towel to keep it clean, leaving the bowl by the edge of the stove to rise.

Bread making is a slow process; it can't be rushed. This is another reason why memories of my grandmother and my childhood bring such comfort. They continue to radiate warmth in my life; it was a simpler, slower time. There was never any need to hurry.

Once the dough had risen to twice its size, she would place it on a floured board and knead again. Her warm hands folded the dough in on itself and her knuckles knew how hard to "punch" it down. The texture became smooth and silky. She then divided the dough into loaves and buns—two loaves for us (my grandfather refused to eat shop-bought bread) and a tray of buns for the next-door neighbor. The loaves and buns would be set by the stove again to rise until small cracks appeared on top; then she would put them in the oven.

By mid-morning, the aroma was intoxicating. I could hardly wait for the loaves and buns to go into the oven. As soon as they were baked, I ran into the kitchen, tore open a piping hot bun and ate it, with no butter! To me they were perfect just as they were.

As years passed, I began to appreciate my grandmother's cooking skills more and more. When we traveled down from Perth on Saturdays to visit her, the journey of 250 kilometers (155 miles) did not seem so long because I knew she would have baked our favorite treats. We traveled every weekend to visit after my grandfather died because she was lonely and increasingly succumbing to Alzheimer's. She began to forget who we were, but she never forgot how to bake bread. She died the year I turned 18–I did not have enough time with her, but the memories of her baking and her kitchen sustain me.

The tragedy of this story is that I do not have her original recipe for bread. I wrote it down a number of times over the years but somehow did not hang onto any copy. I have one of her handwritten recipe books, but as with many of her weekly baked goods—Anzac biscuits, date slice, and pikelets, she never recorded them. So many of her favorites that became my favorites, are missing. It is a testament to her skill as a baker that she remembered intricate and detailed recipes.

Her bread making was not only a necessity; it meant much more to me—it was the bread of love.

White Bread (No. 2)

Makes 2 medium sized loaves and 12 buns.

Adapted from one of the cookbooks in my grandmother's collection, The Golden Wattle Cookery Book *(1960), 16th ed. by E. S. Wigg, Perth, Western Australia.*

3 ½ lb. flour
1 oz. fresh yeast
2 t. sugar
4 c. tepid water
2 t. salt

1. Preheat oven to 100°F. Grease and flour two loaf pans and line baking sheet with parchment.
2. In large basin, sift flour, then warm in oven for about 10 minutes.
3. In small bowl, mix yeast and sugar. Add tepid water and stir.

4. Make well in flour and pour in yeast/sugar/water mixture.
5. On floured board, knead dough about eight to ten minutes until smooth.
6. Place dough on floured basin. Mark with cross. Leave in warm place until dough doubles in size (about one hour).
7. Turn dough out onto floured board. Add salt. Knead until smooth and even, with no holes.
8. Divide mixture into three equal parts (two for loaves, one for buns). Shape two parts into loaf shapes and remainder into 12 pieces for buns. Place loaves in loaf pans and buns on baking sheet.
9. Place in warm place. Allow to rise about 45 minutes. Surface should show small cracks or air bubbles.
10. Bake in hot oven (420°F). Buns take about 30 minutes, loaves about 45.
11. When finished, bread will have hollow sound when tapped on bottom with knuckles. Allow to cool.

MOST OF ALL, I REMEMBER MA

Mildred Pierson Davella

I can still smell Ma's cardamom bread that she made every week. She came to this country from Sweden when she was only 18, not speaking the language and knowing only two family members. She had real guts. Of course, she had to work—first as a maid, then she became a cook in a wealthy home in Providence, Rhode Island, where she learned to make many dishes including oyster stew with lots of butter and cream; this was served for breakfast!

Ma's father was a tenant farmer in Sweden. Her family lived in a one-room cottage. When her mother and father were out, she and her two brothers and sister were fond of roasting bits of pork and chickpeas on the hearth. She told me how delicious they were. Roasting was strictly forbidden in her Lutheran family because fire was thought to be the work of the devil.

Eventually, in this country, she met my father—a chicken farmer—in church and married at the relatively late age of 23. I was the last born of five children—all daughters. My second oldest sister, Dorothy, lived for only 15 months. A jar of phenobarbital was unfortunately too close to her grasp. After she died, my father thought my mother should return to Sweden to see her mother. She traveled by ship with my oldest sister Gertrude. It was the only time Ma saw her mother and homeland again.

My mother was short and fat and looked like a peasant. Until the day she died at 90, she had long hair that fell below her waist. Each morning, she brushed it out, twisted it around the top of her head, and pinned it into

Ida Dahlman Pierson and her baby daughter Mildred. © Mildred Pierson Davella. Used by permission.

place with combs. Then she put on a housedress. When we lived in Minnesota (after Dorothy died, my father became a Swedish Baptist minister and was posted there), she cooked, sewed, and washed all our clothes, made soap and candles, butchered the hogs, laid out the dead in our parlor, fed the chickens, and churned butter. She had a very hard life. It's not surprising that she had a nervous breakdown that kept her hospitalized for some months. During that time, my older sister, Doris, nine at the time, took care of me. I called her *Lille Mor*, Swedish for "Little Mother." She was quite the manager.

I was born in the parsonage in Karlstad, Minnesota, a tiny hamlet of 500 people, 40 miles from the Canadian border. Swedish was spoken at home, and we raised almost all our food, using every bit of the animal once it was slaughtered.

We lived in Minnesota until I was five. Then my father was transferred to a church in Connecticut. There, we lived in the parsonage. At the dining table, my sisters and I loved to get Ma giggling. It wasn't hard. Once she started, she couldn't stop. All the raucous noise drove my father crazy. He liked order and would hold up a wooden spoon, and warn "Peace, peace" until we were able to calm ourselves.

When Ma made her weekly batch of cardamom bread, she used a metal dough maker. This contraption was simply a pail with a crank coming out of the cover that could be turned to do the kneading. Before bedtime, she mixed the dough, placed a pastry board on the kitchen radiator, put the pail on top, covered it with a flour sack, and let it rise slowly overnight. Sometimes it rose too much. Then, in the morning, the dough would be oozing out from under the lid. Ma always made a large batch without a recipe from memory; it would produce a variety of shapes—braids, rolls, and figure eights.

She sprinkled the braids with fresh milk and then coarse sugar before baking, and brushed the *bullar* (rolls) with melted butter while still warm from the oven. When the rolls began to get stale, she cut them in half and dried them in the oven until they were crisp. These *skorpa*, similar to *zwieback*, were good for dunking in cups of aromatic Swedish coffee.

Cardamom Coffee Bread

Makes two braids, about 12 servings per loaf.

I have often made my mother's coffee bread over the years, although not so much anymore. After all, I am 91 years old! Every time I make it and smell that yeasty odor coming from the oven, I remember Ma. I've updated the recipe for a more modern kitchen.

½ c. milk
½ c. sugar
½ stick unsalted butter
½ t. salt
½ c. water, heated to 110°F
2 pkg. active dry yeast (¼ oz. each)
1 t. sugar
2 lg. eggs
½ t. crushed white cardamom pods or ground cardamom
4 c. King Arthur bread flour
Sparkling white sugar

1. In small saucepan, combine first four ingredients; bring to boil, stirring constantly, and then cool to 110°F.
2. In medium bowl, combine warm water with yeast and sugar, cover with pot lid until softened—it will look foamy.
3. In large bowl, using wire whisk, beat eggs until light yellow. Add cardamom and two mixtures from steps 1 and 2. Stir to combine.
4. Using electric mixer fitted with dough hook on low speed, start adding flour, a little at a time, beating well after each addition until flour is fully incorporated and dough is smooth and forms a ball. Sprinkle a little flour on pastry board, and place dough in center. Knead until it doesn't stick either to board or hands, and can be lifted up, about 10 to 12 minutes.
5. Grease mixing bowl with shortening and add dough. Cover with waxed paper or parchment greased with shortening so risen dough will not stick, and cover with towel to keep warm. Allow to rise in warm place until dough has doubled.
6. Grease nine by thirteen-inch metal pan with shortening. Cut dough with knife into two equal pieces. Then cut each half into three equal pieces. Braid dough strands and place both braids crossways in prepared pan. Allow to rise again until when you stick in your finger, the hole remains indented rather than springing back.
7. While dough is rising, preheat oven to 350°F. (Braids will continue to rise while baking.) Brush braids with beaten egg or milk, sprinkle with sparkling white sugar, and bake for 20 to 25 minutes.
8. Watch braids as they bake to see that they become golden brown. If they get too dark, turn down oven. (My mother taught me to test for doneness by taking the pan out of the oven and wrapping my knuckles underneath quickly. If the sound is hollow, it means the braids are baked through.)
9. When done, cover pan with wire rack and quickly invert. Then, using second wire rack, invert again and allow braids to cool.
10. When cool, slice crosswise into half-inch pieces and serve with Swedish coffee, or store in plastic ziplock bags.

Swedish Coffee

Coffee beans
Water
1 egg

1. Crack egg into small custard cup, saving shells, and refrigerate egg for future use.
2. Place eggshell in flame-proof coffeepot.

3. Remaining egg white on shell will make coffee clear and golden.
4. Coarsely grind beans and add to pot along with measured water for desired number of cups.
5. Bring to boil for about five minutes and serve.

CUBAN BREAD PUDDING

Patricia Espinosa-Artiles

At the home of my maternal grandparents, not even the simplest domestic chores escaped the watchful eye of *Papipa*, my great-grandmother. Her name was Paula, but most people called her *Paulita* or Little Paula, which in Spanish connotes affection. When my older brother began to speak, he was unable to pronounce *Paulita* and resorted instead to sounding out the syllables that most resembled what he heard. *Papipa* stuck among the children.

My grandparents lived in Camaguey, a large colonial city in central Cuba. It is common for several generations to live under the same roof. Although not always ideal, this arrangement has the advantage of spreading household chores among a number of people. In our house, this benefit became moot; duties were distributed, but *Papipa* ruled over every detail.

When I turned one, my parents moved to Ciego de Avila, about 100 kilometers (62 miles) west of Camaguey. During the next ten years we traveled to visit *Papipa* at least once a month. But the anticipation of the visits was nothing compared to the excitement of extended summer vacations. As soon as the school year ended, my brother and I traveled to Camaguey to spend the next two months in total bliss. This was the time of year when *Papipa* prepared special drinks, desserts, and succulent meals for us. The fact that my brother and I were, let's say, on the "heavy side," was no deterrent for *Papipa* who insisted we were merely "healthy," a common Cuban euphemism for overweight.

Three particular dishes represented the pinnacle of Cuban cuisine at our family's dinner table. *Arroz con pollo* was a Sunday favorite. This tasty concoction, consisting of rice and chicken pieces sautéed in olive oil with green bell peppers, onions, garlic, cilantro, and tomato sauce, and cooked slowly together in beer, is a Cuban favorite. When beef was available, *Papipa* prepared her delicious version of *carne con papas*, cubes of beef cooked with garlic, olive oil, and chunks of potato. The most reliable fare of Cuban diners, however, is *bistec de puerco* or pork steak. In this dish, pork cutlets, previously marinated in lemon juice and garlic, are grilled and topped with grilled onions. The best part of *Papipa's* exquisite dinners, was, of course, dessert.

There was one object in *Papipa's* kitchen that always attracted me. It was a bag made of cheesecloth in which she kept leftover bread, accumulated throughout the week. *Papipa* hung the bag from a nail hammered high on the wall facing the largest window. By "airing" the bread in this way, she prevented it from getting moldy, a formidable goal in the humidity. I knew that when the bag was full, it would be time for *Papipa* to prepare the most special of all desserts, the weekly bread pudding.

The importance of this dessert owed as much to its great taste as to *Papipa's* strict rules of preparation. The bread had to be as hard as rock. The milk had to be fresh; the simple syrup had to be prepared in the same mold used for baking. This round metal container was used exclusively for bread pudding. The dramatic high point occurred when *Papipa* wrapped the mold in brown-bag paper tied with string and placed it in a water bath (known in Spanish as *baño de María*) on the stove top.

More than 30 years have passed, but the memory of *Papipa's* every kitchen move is as vivid today as if we had seen each other last week. It never occurred to me to ask for the recipe. If I had, I doubt she could have provided measurements. The amount of milk was based on the amount of bread, and the amount of sugar on the volume of bread and milk together, but always more than common sense would suggest. The number of eggs varied, too, but *Papipa* said the right consistency would always require "more than three." There was a *chorrito* (light pouring) of vanilla, and the ultimate key to every excellent dessert, a pinch of salt.

Papipa died when I was 12. By that time, she had initiated me into her unique culinary style. A few years after *Papipa* died, Cuba entered the *período especial*, an extensive "special period" of economic crisis after the break-up of the Soviet bloc signaled the end of economic subsidies to Cuba. It became nearly impossible to gather the ingredients necessary to make bread pudding. Inventive as ever, Cubans began improvising new unlikely versions. There was "one-egg pudding" and "brown sugar pudding," among others. For Cubans, a meal is not complete until you bring something sweet to your lips. And when I say sweet, I mean sweeter than most Americans would find even remotely acceptable.

While living in Cuba as an adult, I attempted several times to make *Papipa's* bread pudding. It was never as good as hers. Maybe it was a sensation fed by nostalgia or maybe the difference was factual. It was only when I came to live in Tucson, Arizona, that I began slowly to trace my way back to *Papipa's* original recipe. It is hard to tell whether my recollections are correct, or whether the sensation of reconnecting with the smells and sounds of my great-grandmother's kitchen has given birth to an original invention that my mind in exile has "cooked up." One thing is certain: the memory of *Papipa* in her kitchen has brought me more than just homesickness; it has also allowed me to invent a new "home" for myself far from the original. For this sweet miracle, I am deeply grateful to my *bisabuela* (great-grandmother).

Cuban Bread Pudding

Serves 4 to 6

Half a loaf French bread (about one-half pound)
½ c. sugar
⅓ c. water
3 eggs, slightly beaten
1 ¼ c. milk
1 t. vanilla
¾ c. sugar
Pinch of salt

1. A few days before making pudding, leave bread out to dry.
2. Preheat oven to 325°F.
3. In small heavy pan over medium heat, prepare *caramelo* (caramel) by stirring sugar with water with wooden spoon. When sugar turns deep amber color, pour on bottom of 1 qt. soufflé dish and quickly swirl up sides.
4. Crumble bread roughly by hand or in food processor. In large bowl, mix bread, milk, sugar, eggs, vanilla and salt. Stir well.
5. Pour mixture into prepared soufflé dish inserted into baking pan. Add boiling water 2 inches up sides of dish, lay piece of foil over dish, and bake for 1 hour. Pudding is done when toothpick inserted in center comes out clean.
6. Remove mold from water bath and leave out at room temperature for two hours, then refrigerate for two to three hours or overnight. When cool, unmold pudding onto serving plate.

MY MOTHER'S *CHILAQUILES*

Meredith E. Abarca

Frying corn tortillas and onions on one burner, sizzling red tomatoes, serrano chiles, and garlic on another, followed by the aroma of coriander, the soft taste of *queso fresco* (soft fresh cheese) and the smoothness of *crema* (Mexican sour cream) is a sensory embrace that warms my soul. These are the basic ingredients of what my mother calls, "*la comida de los pobres*" (the food of the poor): *chilaquiles*. This simple peasant Mexican dish has enriched my mother's life as well as mine. While I was raised eating *chilaquiles* from the time I was three, I did not learn of my mother's knowledge embedded in food until I became an adult and began to cook, guided by her spirit.

When I want to feel my mother's closeness, despite the 1,000 miles between our homes—hers in Menlo Park, California, and mine in El Paso, Texas—I make *chilaquiles*. Thanks to her example, I know to buy the thinnest tortillas, as they fry more evenly, something she learned by making her own. As the wonderful smell of frying tortillas engulfs my home, my mother's life story keeps me company, reminding me of a history that runs through my veins—the story of a fighter.

My mother, Liduvina Vélez known as Duvi, was born on June 24, 1941, on the small ranch of Tepalcatepec in Michoacan, Mexico. She was the oldest of three girls. By the time she was eight, her parents divorced, and the daughters' lives took different paths. The youngest stayed with her father; the middle one went to live with a maternal aunt; my mother ventured out on her own. Since this early age, she has had to figure out how to survive, first on her own, then within two destructive marriages, and eventually as a single mother, raising seven children. Food, or better yet, *la comida de los pobres,* has been both her sail and anchor, allowing her to navigate life's passages from teenaged wife, to single mother, to empowering presence when I share her story at national and international academic conferences.

By the time my mother married at not quite 16, she had already acquired substantial culinary experience—which served as a catalyst for charting paths of self-assurance.

Tortillas are the first ingredient needed to make *chilaquiles*. Since my mother lived on a ranch for years, she knew that a tortilla's quality begins with preparation of the soil, planting seeds of corn, and cultivating the field. She knew that the tender ears must be left on the plant until they dry up. At that point, the cobs are picked and their kernels scraped off.

These are then boiled in water with lime (*cal*) so the hulls slip off. Once the kernels are cooked, they are drained, and ground for *masa* (dough) for tortillas. To fashion white, flavorful tortillas, my mother knew it was crucial not to overdo the lime. Otherwise, the kernels turn yellow and the *masa* has a tingling taste, ruining both aesthetics and flavor. My mother also learned to make thin, perfectly round tortillas. Thinness is important for *chilaquiles* since the strips fry better and retain less oil.

All this practice gave my mother an advantage over her mother- and sisters-in-law. Perhaps following the custom of the time, she lived with her in-laws the first years of her matrimonial life. At the in-laws, she was made to feel an unwelcome guest. Her cooking ability, however, allowed her to claim a space of respect. Her tortillas were perfect compared to those of these female relatives.

Living on a ranch also allowed my mother to develop an appreciation for food's natural and fresh taste. Two other key ingredients in *chilaquiles* are cheese and cream. My mother's culinary palate holds the memory of these dairy products that began with milking a cow and ended with the satisfaction of eating chemically unaltered foods. My mother's farming skills gave her a sense of pride in preparing *la comida de los pobres* with the best quality pre-made products that her minimal financial resources could afford, once she no longer fashioned them from scratch.

Poverty, coupled with the need to feed, dress, and educate her children, drove my mother to make her living by preparing and selling *la comida de los pobres*, including *chilaquiles*. Thanks to her culinary abilities, she attracted a loyal clientele. The self-esteem she gained from earning an income and supporting her children on her own, free of an abusive husband, opened a world of possibilities.

Now that my mother and I live in the United States in urban settings, it is difficult to grow corn and certainly impossible to keep a cow. But I do grow tomatoes, coriander, serrano chiles, green onions, and garlic—the other ingredients for *chilaquiles*. When I walk into my kitchen with a bowl of fresh edibles, I experience the same pride my mother did when she made this dish from scratch, a pride that reminds us of our connection to nature.

Nowadays, for my mother and me, a plateful of *chilaquiles* has a number of meanings. At one level, it represents our love for each other, as she fixes them for me when I visit her, and I fix them for her when she visits me. But the idea of *chilaquiles* has become the compass for my academic journey. When I write about my mother's *chilaquiles*, I capture the accomplishments of not only one peasant Mexican woman, but many more. When I share her culinary knowledge, I not only honor her, but also offer a tribute to others who have found spiritual nourishment in *la comida de los pobres*: *chilaquiles*.

Duvi's *Chilaquiles*

Thin small corn tortillas (2 to 3 per person)
1 medium onion
2 to 3 plum tomatoes, halved
2 to 3 serrano chiles
2 to 3 cloves garlic, peeled
Handful of cilantro
½ c. *queso fresco* (Mexican fresh cheese), crumbled
¼ c. Mexican *crema* (or sour cream)
½ to 1 c. vegetable oil
Salt to taste

1. Cut tortillas into quarter-inch strips.
2. In large, heavy saucepan over medium-high heat, warm few tablespoons (two to four) oil. When oil is hot, drop in tortilla strip; if it sizzles, oil is ready. Drop in handful of tortilla strips and fry to golden color, but not brown. Remove to platter lined with paper towels and sprinkle with salt. Continue until all tortilla strips are fried, drained, and salted.

Tomato Sauce

1. Pour off oil from saucepan. Add two tablespoons clean oil. When hot, add tomatoes, chiles, and garlic. Cook five to six minutes, stirring occasionally. Transfer to blender, adding cilantro. Chop on medium speed for few minutes.
2. In same saucepan, add one tablespoon oil. Dice half of onion and sauté until translucent. Add tomato sauce. Cook few minutes. Add fried tortilla strips. Mix well. Add cheese crumbles. Cover until cheese melts (three to four minutes).
3. To serve, place generous portion *chilaquiles* on individual plates, sprinkle with more cheese, *crema*, few slices avocado, and raw onion.

While you eat, remember a mother's knowledge!

ALLA EGGS

Susan J. Leonardi

My Sicilian grandmother, Guiseppa LaRossa Leonardi (Josephine to her Italian-American friends, Ma to us), grew herbs in her garden in Los Angeles, made her own pasta, and understood that several cloves of garlic would improve almost any dish. Although I spent my childhood clinging to my other Grandma (who, unlike Ma, spoke perfect English, didn't scream, didn't feign heart attacks when she felt underappreciated, and thought I was terrific), I couldn't resist the pull of Ma's cooking.

Ma didn't like me much. I didn't have an Italian mother, and spoke only English. Her other grandchildren were 100 percent Italian and in control of at least the rudiments of her native language. But I was the one who always held out my bowl for more pasta, and I was the biggest fan of her cookies.

I don't remember seeing her make the dough. Once in a while, she'd still be shaping it when we arrived. Usually by the time we got to her house in a corner of Los Angeles, there would be a big pail of cookies covered with a towel in the kitchen. You could eat one—or two or three—whenever you wanted, because unlike other cookies, these were good for you.

"Alla eggs," Ma insisted when my weight-conscious mother and aunts protested. "Nothing bad. No fat. Alla eggs."

The cookies were hard. The cookies were dry. But once you started eating them, you couldn't stop. If you dunked them in coffee, milk or red wine, oh, heaven.

Some of the cookies were plain. Some had nuts. Some had frosting. Ma made them large, she made them small; she made them shaped like tiny footballs. Some she rolled long between her palms and then formed into Ss. For Susan? I wondered. Yes, Ma said, if I asked aloud. "For you."

Occasionally, my mother would ask for the recipe. Ma would shrug. And then say, again, "Alla eggs."

Well, that was a start, I thought, when I determined—years after Ma died and I had long since made my peace with olive skin, peasant stock, and all things Italian—that I would learn to make them. By this time, I looked back with shame and dismay on that callous, callow girl who never asked her grandmother a thing about her life. What was it like, Ma, to travel from Sicily to the United States alone at 16? What was it like to sell cigars in Detroit? To lose two small children to smallpox, before setting off again (prompted by a Mafia hit right in the street) for more hospitable terrain? What was it like to live among strangers, struggle with language, to be unable to read even your native tongue? No wonder that smart-alecky Susan, who found you embarrassing, wasn't the child of your heart.

So perhaps the determination to replicate the cookies was a way to apologize, to connect, to find common ground—even though it was much too late—with this woman I now found brave and compelling. I knew there must have been a modicum of sugar in those cookies (though they were not very sweet), a pinch of leavening, a dash of salt, some flour, and whatever extra flavoring Ma was in the mood for—anise, vanilla, almond, chocolate. In other words, they were the simplest of cookies, like biscotti but without the bother of the second baking. I set about experimenting. Some tries were better than others, but they all worked, more or less. Sometimes I find in the pages of one cookbook or another, a slip of paper in my handwriting headed "Ma's Cookies." No two are the same.

If I make them for friends and they ask me for the recipe, I shrug and say, "Alla eggs."

Ma's Cookies

Makes about 2 dozen

This recipe calls for almond extract. You can, of course, vary the flavoring and additions, just as Ma did. For example, use a teaspoon of vanilla extract instead of, or in addition to, almond. Use chocolate bits or dried cherries in addition to, or in place of, almonds. If you want fancy, frost with a simple glaze of powdered sugar, warm water, and vanilla extract or cocoa.

2 eggs
⅓ c. sugar
1 ½ c. organic white flour
¼ t. baking soda
⅛ t. salt
½ t. almond extract
¼ c. finely chopped almonds.

1. Preheat oven to 375°F. Lightly grease two cookie sheets.
2. In medium bowl, beat eggs with whisk until blended. Gradually add sugar, beating as you go. Add almond extract.
3. Combine flour, baking soda, and salt in small bowl. Add dry mixture to eggs. Stir in almonds. Dough should be stiff enough to handle with floured hands. If too sticky, add more flour, one tablespoon at a time. Break off one-inch pieces of dough and form into logs, footballs, or make ropes for Ss. Place cookies one inch apart on baking sheets.
4. Bake 20 minutes, or until cookies are lightly browned and quite hard. Cool on dish towels placed on wire racks. Dunk in coffee, red wine, or milk.

DINNER IN THE NIXON WHITE HOUSE

Janet Chrzan

As for my mother's cooking (God bless her in the Great Kitchen in the Sky), she was from the Upper Peninsula of Michigan. Enough said, eh?

I've always suspected that she possessed a deflavorizing device rather than an oven. At least the results indicated so.

Her best dish—which she developed in Northern California in the 1970s—is one I gladly share, if only so the true horrors of her cooking can be known. Actually, this dish was very good, and did not involve use of the oven. It was a stove-top creation in the best tradition of 1970's cuisine, a spaghetti sauce (made with minute attention to the Lawry's spaghetti seasoning packet recipe), combined with frozen hamburger. Don't ask me why the meat had to be frozen; my mother had an elaborate ritual of carefully frying it, scraping off each successive layer as it became brown and presumably defrosted. She then added (exactly as per the packet) canned tomato puree, canned tomato paste, contents of the (euphemistically-speaking) seasoning packet, and a small can or two of sliced mushrooms. All was then left to burn a bit in the cast-iron skillet while she boiled the vermicelli (she never used thick spaghetti strands) for about an hour until nicely soft.

So here are the details for Spaghetti in the Nixon White House, a recipe that continues my narrative: This spaghetti is actually surprisingly good; so good that I requested it as my birthday meal every year . . . the rest of it should be consigned to the appropriate 1970's level of Dante's hell– the place where mirrored faux-gold-streaked hallways still exist, where lime-green flowered contact paper is used EVERYWHERE, and the cultural mythology demands that happy families gather nightly to play "THE GAME OF LIFE." This would be a long, long time before your only daughter becomes an honest-to-god ACLU-card totin' pagan liberal!

Spaghetti à la the Nixon White House

Serves 4

1 Lawry's spaghetti sauce seasoning packet, purchased from Safeway supermarket
1 lb. frozen hamburger meat, preferably in a square shape for easy browning, selected from the supermarket freezer after it has been reduced to $.39 pound. (Oops, I just dated myself, didn't I?)
2 cans tomato puree, generic Safeway brand
1 can Safeway tomato paste
1 or 2 cans mushroom slices, or mushroom pieces if you're feeling a bit poor or your husband has just found out what you spent at Safeway last month
1 lb. generic Safeway brand white flour vermicelli

1. Add frozen meat right from freezer to large cast-iron skillet over medium heat. Brown successively on all sides until reduced to pile of cooked hamburger nubbins, floating in copious grease (because you bought the lowest-priced hamburger). Drain grease, or at least some (this is a sop to millennium sensibilities).

2. Return hamburger to skillet. Add tomato paste and puree, contents of seasoning packet, and mushrooms. Stir a bit and cook over low heat as long as you like.

3. Fill large saucepan with water, add salt, and bring to boil. Break up full pound of vermicelli into smallish pieces, and add to pot. Alternately, if you're feeling like taking a walk on the dangerous ethnic side, drop pasta in unbroken. Then you have to be prepared to use spoon and fork and swirl it when you eat, which is not something most Presbyterians know how to do. Boil pasta for a long time. Who knows? It might be like pork–if underdone, you could develop "trichiwhatsis" and die.

4. While pasta and sauce are cooking, drink large martini and eat canned black olives filled with cream cheese. Your husband will drink two martinis, accompanied by most of a bag of ridged potato chips, dipped in a curious sauce made from IMO fake sour cream and Lipton's onion soup. Have a spirited discussion about what a fine fellow Billy Graham is, how that nice man Nixon is getting a bum deal, and how terrible that all those damned illegal Mexicans working in agriculture in our area of northern California can get food stamps, taking money out of the pockets of good hardworking WHITE Americans who know how to WORK for a dollar, by God!

5. Drain pasta and add to tomato meat sauce. Let cook for another hour while you and your husband drink more martinis and talk about those damned welfare cheats, how awful and grasping and show-offy the neighbors are with their new fancy car, how the boss at work is a dirty so-and-so, and how Lawrence Welk always has such a nice old-timey, good Christian show every week, but that most of the rest of TV programming is garbage and wouldn't be allowed if the Birchers were in political power like they should be, since most TV is controlled by Jews and the Trilateral Commission, a kind of trade and philanthropy group, the Davos of the '70s.

6. Serve the vaguely burned, dried-out pile of noodles and sauce with four salad plates of iceberg lettuce chunks, three rock-hard tomato wedges, and two canned, black olives. Drench in store-bought bleu cheese dressing and lots of salt.

7. If you happen to be again feeling dangerously ethnic and are prepared to battle the demons of your Calvinist, Scottish ancestors (who spend an inordinate amount of time spinning in their graves), serve the meal with a–GASP–bottle of Chianti, last week's vintage, artfully covered in a woven-basket chastity belt with dangerously inadequate-looking thinly-plaited handles.

8. Serve canned fruit salad for dessert.

BISCUITS AND GRAVY

Kristen Miglore

I grew up marveling at the oddities that filled my grandmother's home in east Los Angeles—her miniature animal collection, the cufflinks and half-full aftershave bottles that stood on the bathroom counter long after my grandpa died, the 1911 warbly, white piano. For the 23 years she lived there without him, the haunted old house bustled and breathed with Grandmother—a name much too prim for a woman so brash and loving. She'd paint my nails anytime I asked, playfully threaten to "beat me upside the head" when I was bad, and fed me gloriously rich, homey food every chance she got.

Kristen Miglore's grandmother Grace Cowan in a family kitchen in Santa Barbara, California just after Grace moved into a nearby retirement community. © Kristen Miglore. Used by permission.

Her cooking remains thoroughly Southern, always a comfort to a kid raised on egg substitute and skim milk in the 1980s. Dinner at Grandmother's was lush, beefy oxtail stew or fried pork steak with her trademark mayonnaise-laced potato salad. For breakfast, she'd fry up hog jaw, a meat whose uninviting name and scrappy appearance I could overlook as long as it was served next to a stack of her buttery Wonder Bread French toast. But the most iconic meal at Grandmother's still is biscuits and gravy.

Her biscuits are small and golden, with a thin crust of oily crunch sheltering a steaming, fluffy interior. We tear them in half crosswise and douse them with thick, creamy gravy—milky-sweet and flecked with black pepper and bits of scrambled egg. After several rounds of gravy-sodden biscuits, the final one is always consumed sweet. I followed Grandmother's lead, mashing up a paste of honey and whipped butter to apply the final decadent touch.

Grandmother always serves her biscuits and gravy with a meaty companion known as fresh side—slices of pork dredged in flour and fried crisp. Like bacon, it comes from the flesh along the pig's ribs, but is uncured and retains the rind, which I only recently learned is the pig's skin. Once fried, the rind is edible though very tough, so you can either gnaw on it (like Grandmother does) or feed it to the dog (like I do). Much more than a side dish, this meat acts as both the base for the gravy's roux and a crispy, satisfyingly al dente foil to the fluff and slop on the rest of the plate. I'm convinced it's the savory drippings from the shallow-fried fresh side that elevate Grandmother's gravy above all the best "home-style" restaurant renditions, most of which rely on crumbled sausage.

Though fresh side has been invariably wedded to biscuits and gravy in my lifetime, Grandmother recently told me that during the Depression, her family could only afford, in her words, "water biscuits and water gravy." She learned this unsavory formula when she was 11 and tasked with feeding her seven younger siblings. She has been cooking more tempting versions ever since, first for her husband and three daughters, then grandchildren, and now her grandchildren's friends—towed from far corners of California to her kitchen specifically for the meal.

She doesn't live in her L.A. house anymore, having reluctantly traded it in for a bright, sensible apartment in a retirement community in Santa Barbara. No longer surrounded by artifacts from her marriage, she keeps Grandpa alive in other ways. She boasts of the monuments his steel company built, recites his classic drink order ("CC7, tall, with a chunk of lime")—and has even started crediting her gravy to him.

It was his idea, she insists, to scramble eggs into the sauce before thickening. To his credit, the eggs are important, adding heft and texture. Without them, it wouldn't be the same—but still delicious. I have studied the way she puts this meal together by heart so I can do the same. I won't be convinced that the recipe isn't hers. But since she honors his contribution, however small, I will too.

The last time I visited her, she was recovering from a fall and, for once, I took care of her. We were both dismayed by her sudden frailty, but her brassy sense of humor kept our spirits up. Cautiously pushing her walker through the apartment, her left side swollen and purple, she'd announce, "Here I go . . . Miss America!" and "Watch out, reckless driver!"

I cooked all our meals, even frying hog jaw for the first time with her hollering instructions from the next room. As we tried to eat the scraps I had seared into salty leather, she offered, "You stay here long enough and I'll teach you how to cook the old fashioned way." At least with biscuits and gravy, I've long been a disciple. Mine aren't perfect yet, but I'm almost ready to try them on her.

Grandmother's Biscuits and Gravy

Makes 6

My grandmother never measures anything, not even Bisquick. Try not to smirk at the ready-made mix—it's delicious. When I've indulged my inner food idealist and made biscuits from scratch, they have rarely tasted as good and always take longer to make.

Bisquick
Milk, preferably whole or 2%
Flour
Vegetable oil
24 slices fresh side, or pork belly (if fresh side is unavailable)
Salt and pepper
4 eggs

1. Preheat oven to 450°F. Pour Bisquick into large bowl and add milk, stirring until dough comes together but is still thick. Turn out dough onto well-floured surface. Using rolling pin or hands, press out dough to one-half-inch thick. Cut out biscuits with a two-and-one-half-inch biscuit cutter.
2. Drizzle oil into high-sided baking pan (my grandmother always uses eight by eight-inch) and rub each biscuit in oil as you place in pan, turning to coat all sides. Biscuits should touch at edges. Bake about 12 minutes or until golden.

3. Over medium heat, warm large frying pan. Add enough oil to coat bottom generously. Salt and pepper each piece of fresh side, back and front, and dredge in flour, shaking off excess. Place pieces in pan in single layer. Fry until golden brown on both sides, turning with tongs as needed. Remove slices and drain on paper towels.

4. Pour off all but thin layer of oil. Over medium heat, crack eggs into pan one at a time, scrambling as you go. Season with salt and pepper. Once eggs are soft scrambled, sprinkle in flour. Continue to stir as you brown flour lightly, adding more oil if necessary.

5. Pour in milk slowly, stirring continuously. Simmer gravy, stirring occasionally until thickened. If too thin, mix together small amount of flour and water and add. Season gravy with salt and pepper to taste.

6. Transfer gravy to serving bowl and biscuits to basket, and serve along with fresh side plus honey, butter, and jams.

CAKEWALK

Renee Marton

Making lemon cheesecake—preparing it, baking it, and eating it—is one of my family traditions. From my grandmother to my mother, to my brother and me, making cheesecake was required for special events when I was growing up. My two teenaged nieces continue this tradition today, bringing a fourth generation into the mix.

"Making cheesecake" is my way of embodying a family ideal. Shared behavior between generations produces different special kinds of memories, some stored in our physical selves. Family recipe enactments are similar to little dances, taking place on a culinary stage. When I prepare a family recipe, particularly in a kitchen that I know well, I find that my actions fulfill personal, cultural, and even physical expectations.

My mother, like many women of her generation (she is 83), cooked from index cards with handwritten or printed recipes on them—stained, with notes in the margins—that were usually filed away in boxes or binders. My own recipes are stored in my computer—which I don't think of yet in such a personal way. There will be no box of yellowed clippings for anyone to go through, not even a tattered bunch of index cards. Perhaps that is why I cherish culinary memorabilia not only for recipes, but for the memories and images they evoke. A stained page, or bent index card, begins to flesh out a memory, literally by its existence.

When I cook from memory, several ways of remembering bring the recipe components to my mind and body. Think of a pie; each slice represents a different kind of memory: verbal, visual, and physical. The more I repeat the motions of "making cheesecake," the more my memory stores knowledge as motor or automatic, residing in my body rather than verbal or visual. With practice, the behavior takes place seemingly "without thought." Pouring batter into a crust becomes a stylized movement—a slinky pirouette, after much practice. Eventually, picking up the mixing bowl full of batter triggers all the next "steps" in the right sequence without conscious awareness. To write down this process uses far more words and requires much more detail than simply enacting it after years of practice.

When I was in high school, I would come home and help my mother make dinner at our New York City apartment. She did a lot of baking then and was a pivotal influence on my decision (much later) to become a chef. My cheesecake memories began with her. Miss Balser, as I still call her (her professional and maiden name), would press the buttered and sugared graham cracker crumbs into the springform pan. Then she would add the batter (I licked the bowl), and later, the remains of the topping. Once baked, the cheesecake would separate slightly from the side of the pan, so removal would be easy.

Today, my mother has Parkinson's disease, which has robbed her of her motor skills and motor memory. She can no longer stand unassisted for more than a couple of minutes, and spends her days in a wheelchair. Her hands do not work the way they used to; her left hand is partially crimped over itself, and her right hand has trouble grasping and holding things for very long. Powerlessness does not suit her. Perhaps this is why I like to cook with her. For a moment, we can relive the past, when we shared family cooking rituals in a more equal way than we do now.

So we make cheesecake together in the same apartment where I spent my teen-aged years. She and I embody our family tradition, which we perpetuate in our baking duet. She remembers the ingredients, knows which pans to use, and at what temperature to pre-set the oven. However, she cannot physically put the component parts of the recipe together. She has no way of gaining access to the store of motor memories in her body. I supply them for her. I press the smooth crumb crust into the pan, while my mother stirs the lemon juice (squeezed by me), sugar (measured by me), and sour cream (measured by me) for the topping, in a bowl that I place in her lap. Our mutual sharing leads to a perfect cheesecake—a pas de deux.

Just as a dancer knows the dance without thinking about it, cooks enact a recipe without thinking. Each is a specific dance: the moves required for making each recipe; the pliés and arabesques are choreographed into a ballet that takes place on a kitchen stage. Rehearsing the dance (making the recipe over and over) lays down the motor memory, while tasting the final result reinforces all the processes involved (we hope!). Get out the packages of cream cheese: bend, lift, turn. Place sugar container on the counter, while getting measuring cups out of drawer—one stylized movement. Take the egg carton out of refrigerator, and, one at a time, crack eggs into a bowl—a little tap routine inserted into the main ballet. And so the dance continues until the final bow.

Miss Balser's Lemon Cheesecake

Serves 10 to 12

2 c. graham cracker crumbs
¼ c. sugar
¼ c. melted unsalted butter
Pinch salt

1. Preheat oven to 325°F.
2. Mix ingredients together with wooden spoon until crumbs are well moistened.
3. Press mixture firmly but gently with fingertips into bottom and sides of nine-inch springform pan. Bottom should be smooth and flat, and crumbs should be evenly pressed onto sides. Height of crust should be about one to one and one-half inches from top of pan.
4. Bake for 10 minutes until you can just smell caramel.
5. Remove from oven.

Filling

Three 8 oz. pkgs. Philadelphia cream cheese, softened to room temperature
3 lg. eggs
1 c. sugar
Juice from ½ lemon

1. Using electric mixer on low speed, combine cream cheese and sugar, and blend thoroughly.
2. Add eggs, one at a time, incorporating well, scraping down sides of bowl as needed.
3. Increase mixer speed to medium. Add lemon juice and mix until just combined and smooth with no lumps.

4. Gently pour filling into crust while turning pan in a circle. (If you dump batter in all at once, you may dislodge crust.) Smooth top of filling with back of wooden spoon, if necessary.
5. Bake 40 to 45 minutes, until sides are lightly puffed, and center jiggles slightly. Halfway through, turn pan around halfway for even baking.
6. Remove from oven.

Topping

One 16 oz. container sour cream
¼ c. sugar
Juice from ½ lemon

1. Whisk all ingredients together until well blended.
2. Pour topping gently over cheesecake, starting at outer edge, working toward center. Be gentle to avoid tearing surface. Smooth top with rubber spatula.
3. Return to oven and bake for another 10 minutes. Allow cheesecake to cool on wire rack to room temperature for two hours; then chill overnight before removing from pan. Make sure crust has completely separated from side before unlatching spring. Cut into slices and serve.

DUMPLING MADNESS

Betty Teller

Dumpling. I can't help but smile when I say it. The very word means love and comfort to me, so no wonder I have been hunting for the perfect dumpling my whole life. Steamed dumplings, fried dumplings, chicken and dumplings . . . all any restaurant has to do to assure I'll pick a dish is to put "dumplings" somewhere in the description.

My obsession is rooted in childhood.

My great-grandmother on my father's side doted on me. But she died when I was four, so my only memories of her are fleeting. If it weren't for photographs, I probably wouldn't know what she looked like. But I do have one indelible recollection.

I was at a relative's beach house in Beach Haven, New Jersey, and this wonderful lady is standing at a stove, making dumplings, as many as I can gobble. The most delicious dumplings in the world. Delicate, slightly chewy, child-sized dumplings. The essence of dumpling-ness. The Holy Grail of dumplings. The dumplings I have been searching for forever since.

Alas, the secret of those delectable tidbits was not passed on to my mother. I don't recall her ever making them, or anything like them. And none of my sisters remembers ever having eaten them.

So for 50 years my search has mostly been in restaurants. And I have eaten some seriously disgusting dishes in my quest. I recall with a shudder a particularly dreadful one in Prague 15 years ago. I had such high hopes. I associate dumplings with Eastern European food, and there I was right on the spot. "This could be it!" I thought when I spotted dumplings on the menu.

Then my dish arrived. A large, dense, heavy, steamed glob of tough and strangely textured starch, so big it had actually been sliced into small, indigestible rounds. I nearly cried. It had to be a mistranslation, I convinced myself. And such is the power of the word "dumpling" over my emotions that I actually rationalized ordering it again, when I saw dumplings on the menu at a different restaurant, a few days later. With identical results.

The poor Czechs. I feel sorry for any country that has such wretched dumplings, and after these disappointments, I gave up the search for a long time.

One day, not very long ago, I was dining in an upscale eatery here in Napa, California, and noticed some pasta-like squiggles on the plate. But they weren't pasta. They were more like—dumplings! Though not quite the same, they were closer than anything I had tried in years of searching. I grabbed the menu back to figure out what I was eating. It was *spaetzle*.

The blinders dropped from my eyes. My great-grandmother was German. Of course her dumplings were *spaetzle*!

I was so excited; I couldn't wait to make them. I quickly found numerous recipes on the Web, and also information about *spaetzle* makers—an inexpensive, metal contraption for making nice even squiggles. I bought one and started experimenting in my home.

The first batches were pretty good—I was clearly on the right track. But they didn't ring the memory chimes. I kept trying, working my way through the variations. Then I found a recipe that was a bit different. It contained lard. That made sense—great-grandma wasn't from the Jewish side of the family, so I tried it. And bingo! I was transported.

I called my father, excited to tell him that after years of work I had finally decoded this deep mystery from my childhood, his grandmother's dumplings.

"Dad," I cried. "I figured out that they weren't dumplings at all—they were *spaetzle*!"

"Yes, of course they were," he agreed in a completely unexcited tone. Clearly, he had known all along. Why hadn't he told me? Did he not know of my epic search!?! I thought about Prague and contemplated strangling him.

But I still had my final discovery to convey. "I've figured out how to make them!" I said.

"That's nice," said my father. "You know her secret was lard."

Great-Grandma Spielberger's *Spaetzle*

Serves 4, or one hungry three-year-old

Now that I have finally eaten my fill of spaetzle, I have to acknowledge that the flavor of the basic dumpling is bland—perfect for a three-year-old, and a nice substitute for pasta under a rich sauce, but perhaps not quite sophisticated enough for an adult who isn't trying to recapture a childhood memory. So I have been experimenting with herbs and seasonings. My favorites so far are these, with dill. They're good as is, and would also stand up to a sauce.

1 egg
1 T. lard, melted and cooled (yes, you can substitute butter if you must)
½ c. milk
1 ¼ c. flour
¼ t. baking powder
½ t. salt
¼ t. (or more) fresh ground pepper
½ t. nutmeg, grated fresh
1 T. dried dill (or substitute finely chopped fresh dill, chives, or other fresh herbs)
Special equipment: *Spaetzle* maker (look online for sources or at a cooking utensil store; this is much easier than forcing dough through a colander which is the alternative)

1. Using electric mixer on low, blend together egg, milk, and lard or butter. (Make sure fat has cooled enough after melting so it will not curdle egg.)
2. Using wooden spoon, mix dry ingredients, then add to liquid ingredients and beat with electric mixer until well blended. This will produce something halfway between thick batter and dough.
3. Bring large pot of salted water (six to eight cups) to a boil. Spoon about half dough into *spaetzle* maker. Slide top piece back and forth until all dough has gone through holes into water. When little dumplings are floating (a matter of seconds), they're done. Remove with slotted spoon or strainer—a flat Chinese wire basket strainer works well. Repeat with remaining dough.
4. Toss *spaetzle* with bit of butter, serve plain, or under sauce.

VIRGINIA'S WEARY WILLIE

Marty Martindale

Weary Willie, an early hobo character, originated as a cartoon in 1895, starred in silent movies, and later became a loveable circus clown. However, in our home, Weary Willie was a plain, no-nonsense white cake, and we ate it often.

My mother, Virginia, grew up in a comfortable home where her folks encouraged their maid to prepare many of Thomas Jefferson's favorite dishes. Virginia graduated from Women's College at Brown University with majors in English and economics. Things went well until she dropped out of Columbia University grad school and made an ill-advised marriage to a New Hampshire farmer. Quite soon she found herself a single mom, well before it was a popular option, raising me in a tenement in Providence, Rhode Island. The year was 1936. Ours was the only area apartment with a copy of Tolstoy's *War and Peace* alongside a dark red copy of Agnes Jacques' *A Russian Primer.*

Virginia was not a cake-carrying church lady, but when she baked, it was usually her Weary Willy Cake, a recipe she received from a friend. She knew it by heart. It wasn't so much that Willie was delicious; it was that Willie was easy. She wasn't into upside-down cakes, Lady Baltimores, tomato soup cakes, pudding cakes, or any of the "Surprise Cakes." For rare, fancy occasion cakes she turned to Fannie Farmer. Most post-Depression homes had no Mixmasters for whipping up high, airy cakes.

Virginia called our small cooking area the pantry. In this pantry, she made her Weary Willies, performing what this kid believed was magic. Her magic occurred when her oven changed her soupy mixture into something bread-like I could hold in my fingers! This is how the Willie came together. Virginia had some evidence we were descended from the flour Pillsburys, so it was always important we use Pillsbury flour. She used her displacement method for measuring Crisco by placing one-third cup cool water in a measuring cup. Then she spooned Crisco into the cup until the water line reached two-thirds cup. After she dumped the water, she had an exact one-third cup. For leavening, she used Rumford baking powder from nearby Rumford, Rhode Island, where the giant baking powder can served as both water storage and advertising. Salt was always Worcester brand and granulated sugar was Domino's. Our certified, unpasteurized milk came from Fairoaks Farm. Big fresh eggs came from the weekly egg man to whom my mother enjoyed serving coffee and probably over time, pieces of Willie, topped with her latest courageously-concocted icing.

From my delicate balancing position on the edge of the lower cupboard door, I watched the whole operation including the last ingredient, which went into the Willie. It was Burnett's vanilla.

"What's that for?" I'd ask each time.

She always responded, "To make it taste better."

Toward the end of our cake-baking wonder days, I found I needed to climb up onto the pantry counter, slide carefully across the edge of the sink, reach into the cupboard, and take a big taste of what made cakes taste so much better.

Bitter!

I never asked what vanilla did for a cake again. I wonder if she noticed.

My mother was a person of clean habits; however, it was a family thing to test a cake for doneness with a straw broken from our broom. When each Willie finally came out of our apartment-sized Glenwood range, she inverted it onto our wiggly, wire cake rack. Once cooled and frosted, each Willie went into our round, lidded tin box. Here Virginia practiced one more bit of her magic. About the second day, she'd place a piece of fresh bread into the box with the cake, and lo and behold, the next day the bread was rigid and stale, *and* the cake took on new moisture!

Virginia's Willies were basic, but her frostings at times stunned our not-too-imaginative neighbors. She found the basic powdered, confectioners' sugar recipe easy, and it gave her a chance to vary flavors widely with lemon or orange rind, not yet called zest, sometimes combined with chocolate. These were in addition to her furry coconut, nutty Vermont maple flavor, smooth peanut butter, or fruit jam flavors. Her favorite frosting was her delightfully pink version made with fresh pomegranate juice, a rare fruit for 1936, especially in North America.

Weary Willie Cake

1 egg, broken into a measuring cup, fill remainder with whole milk
⅓ c. Crisco
1 ½ c. flour
Pinch of salt
2 t. baking powder
1 c. flour (my mother used regular flour; she couldn't afford cake flour)
1 t. vanilla

1. Preheat oven to 350°F.
2. In medium bowl, combine dry ingredients.

3. In separate bowl, combine wet ingredients.
4. Add dry ingredients to wet ingredients alternately in thirds, incorporating well after each addition. Bake until broom straw comes out clean, about 30 minutes.

As we explore our relationships with mothers, grandmothers, and great-grandmothers, we mine our memory material for clues about where we've been. This spiritually nourishing reflection serves as a fulfilling touchstone throughout our lives, a reference point for moving on.

2

Lost Times and Places

Leafing idly through certain of these books is like leafing through old diaries; the other evening, half seriously, she'd told Ian that, when they were both old, really old, elderly, they might read these entries aloud to each other; and certain meals, certain days in their lives and evenings with friends, entire pockets of lost time, might be returned to them; as in Proust.[1]
—Joyce Carol Oates, *American Appetites*

There is a magic worked by certain dishes that bring to life entire bygone worlds. Although we can never truly return to these domains, they can be resurrected through the sensory experience of food. Scenarios of life in a summer mountain community, foods served during hardscrabble times, and during prosperous past periods on a tropical island nation are indelibly ingrained parts of our heritage. Food has an uncanny ability to access these deep memories that may be double-edged, recalling the inhumanity of slavery, the displacement of American Indians and the devastating consequences of war. These re-connections to the histories that shaped us form another crucial layer of our identities.

ZEMEL

Carol Durst

Zemel brings me back to a summer during the 1950s in the southern Catskill Mountains, New York. My family was visiting my father's clan. We were all staying in the old, tipsy clapboard house on Uncle Willie's property. Willie had been born in the house. Later, he built the solid stone and brick place where he and Aunt Tillie, my father's sister, raised their four sons and daughter.

The "boys" were all married adults by this summer. The three local ones all came "home" for lunch, sliding into the booth around the table, tormenting Aunt Tillie until she produced sufficient hot food, perhaps fresh-baked *zemel* for dessert.

Zemel is a yeast-raised dough, rolled around cinnamon sugar and raisins, much like *rugelach*, except it is not made from cream cheese dough. *Zemel* might be a Yiddish term derived from the German, "Semmel," a sweet bun, or it might be an invented word, bastardized from Russian and Yiddish.

Aunt Tillie learned baking on the farm in the '20s, where her parents and Willie's—as well as over 500 other East European farmers—took in boarders during the summer. My father told us of his work milking cows, washing up to be the breakfast waiter, cleaning the dining room, and then heading into town for groceries for the next meals. His sisters Tillie and Sadie baked, washed dishes, made beds, and helped their mother.

On a wood-burning stove, my grandmother prepared three meals a day for 30–50 guests, who came to "the Catskills" for their health, specifically to avoid tuberculosis and gain weight. As teenagers, my Aunts Sadie and Tillie baked homey calorie-laden desserts, which allowed for flexible timing, so dough could rise while they made the beds or ingredients could be adjusted if my father was late coming back from the grocer's in White Lake. My father's brothers helped with farm chores and, as soon as they got driver's licenses, worked in long-distance trucking and taxi services. Aunt Sadie was married by 16 and left to start a family. Tillie married Willie and began to raise her family in nearby Monticello.

She developed skills as a baker, learning when the dough needed more flour, more moisture, more time to rise. She used farm produce, eggs, and dairy items; there was always fresh whipped cream to hide a burned spot. Yeast-raised dough with the rich moisture of sour cream was easier to handle on muggy days than more temperamental cream cheese pastry.

I've always thought there must be a family recipe for *zemel*, but my Grandma never learned to read or write in any language, and what might have been in her daughter Tillie's kitchen was lost when she was moved into assisted living. My mother wrote something down long ago, probably that summer back in the 1950s. She laughed as she read ingredients to me from her crumbling paper, "a glass of milk (meaning 6 ounces), 5 cents' worth yeast, ½ glass sour cream or more, sifted flour, one glass at a time."

My cousin Larry remembers my hanging around the kitchen that summer when I was three "helping" Aunt Tillie. A while back, he began asking me to reproduce his mother's treat. As I develop this recipe, now in the 21st century, I send samples to my cousins Larry, Gary and Alan, hoping to do justice to their memory of Tillie's *zemel* 50 years later. The verdict: they are delighted with the tastings and recall a honey glaze that was not in my mother's notes.

I rest my hand on the soft yeast dough on the counter. I have a visual memory of that country kitchen in the 1950s, helping Aunt Tillie sprinkle on more, still more, cinnamon sugar, tossing handfuls of raisins around. Although I learned professionally to cut *rugelach* from a circle, like pizza wedges, I remember just how to pat and roll this dough into a rectangle, cut it into strips and finally the triangles Aunt Tillie had shown me on her kitchen counter years ago.

In my head, I hear the banter of young men with their mother. I smell yeast and cinnamon sugar baking. Aunt Tillie is moving dishes around the kitchen, talking rapidly with everyone and keeping an eye on the *zemel* dough. I must have stayed in a sweet mood, popping lots of those raisins into my mouth.

Zemel

Makes 70–80
  Breakfast pastry, midday snack, or teatime sweet.

Dough

1 pkg. dry yeast
1 t. sugar
6 oz. milk
½ lb. unsalted butter, 2 sticks
1 c. sugar
1 t. salt
1 t. vanilla extract
½ c. (4 oz.) sour cream
4 lg. eggs
6 to 7 c. flour

Filling

1 to 1 ½ c. sugar, mixed with 4 to 6 t. cinnamon
2 c. dark raisins plumped in boiling water for 1 to 2 minutes and drained
1 to 2 c. chopped nuts (walnuts or pecans)

Topping

2 oz. unsalted butter, melted
1 oz. honey, stirred into melted butter
Cinnamon sugar

To Make Dough

1. Combine yeast, warm water, and one teaspoon sugar until softened and dissolved.
2. In two-quart saucepan over medium heat, scald milk and butter together.
3. Add sugar, salt, and vanilla, and stir to cool slightly. When mixture is tepid, blend in yeast mixture, sour cream and eggs (it will be lumpy).
4. Stir in flour, one cup at a time, into liquids and beat after each addition. Dough will be sticky and elastic.
5. Continue adding flour until dough pulls away from sides of saucepan, somewhere around five to six cups.
6. Transfer dough into lightly floured bowl, cover with clean dish towel, and set aside to rise until doubled (about two hours).

To Make *Zemel*

1. Preheat oven to 350°F.
2. In small bowl, prepare topping by blending melted butter with honey, and set aside.
3. Divide dough into four equal parts. Set one on well-floured pastry board, incorporating about one-quarter cup additional flour so it can be handled without sticking. Press by hand, and with rolling pin, into rectangle about eight by twenty inches.
4. Cover surface with cinnamon sugar and chopped nuts.

5. Using pizza cutter or spatula dipped in flour, cut dough lengthwise into two even strips, then cut strips into triangles zigzagging with wide ends about two inches. Sprinkle generous handful (about a half cup) raisins on triangles.
6. Starting at wide end of triangles, press some raisins onto "bottom" edge of dough which will become center of *zemel*. Roll up from wide to narrow, finishing by tucking point of triangle under bundle.
7. Repeat with remaining three sections of dough.
8. Set each bundle on baking sheet. Use pastry brush dipped in honey-butter mixture lightly on top of each *zemel*. Sprinkle with more cinnamon-sugar.
9. Bake for about 15 minutes or until light gold. They are best served warm.

MY NANA'S GRACE

Jeanette Williams

My Nana and Papa were displaced African Southerners, descendents of slaves, slave masters, and Native Americans. She hailed from Boydon, Virginia, he from Chase City, Virginia. The towns kissed each other, and their romance ensued. When my grandmother decided to move north for work, she moved in with her mother's sister Marion, and my grandfather followed soon after. They were married in my Great Aunt Marion's house and it was there that my grandmother learned how to lovingly prepare her hand-rolled yeast rolls.

My grandparents arrived in the North with tenacity and discipline. Nana and Papa were from a different time; they upheld a commitment to family, to saving, and a community loyalty that is rare today. They both worked early on in various jobs, in factories, on farms, and as day laborers. The small town of Farmingdale, New Jersey, called them, as it did many other displaced southerners; a place comfortable, familiar, and rural; a place with farms to work. They relocated to a three-bedroom home on their employer's farm and gave birth to four children: three girls—Gloria Jean, Lillian Ann, Helen—and one son, Richard. My Aunt Helen would leave us at the early age of 26 in 1967 due to complications from lupus.

During my era, when I was old enough to know, my grandparents had moved from their prior place of servitude and purchased a small modest ranch situated on two acres of coveted land. There, the forest would abound, and creeks ran by our feet on log benches as we enjoyed the depth of the woods, pulling us into its mystery and richness.

This land, this house, would create and unfold beautiful memories for many generations. A garden sat on one acre and each spring until early fall, we

Jeanette's Nana Mary Oliver around 1950. © Jeanette Williams. Used by permission.

would assist my Papa with this garden. A blackberry patch sat to the left side, and a strawberry patch, a Concord grape vine, and peach tree bordered the right. My grandfather had planted a neat row of shrubs at the garden's edge, about 100 feet from the back porch, sectioning his private world. Peaches, strawberries, blackberries, potatoes, cantaloupe, string beans, greens, watermelon, tomatoes, lima beans, corn, okra, peas, and Concord grapes made their way into our hands at harvest time and into my grandmother's kitchen where she would create, preserve, can, freeze, and celebrate our labor.

When I started my own small garden some years ago, I called on my grandparents' ancestral wisdom to guide my hand, for memory to assist me. I remember my grandfather checking each vine, each new growth, watching his gentle seedlings take life and bring forth bounty to feed his family.

I understand now why my resonance is so vastly different from theirs. Two steps away from their generation, my grandparents worked land for others, and they watched their parents and grandparents toil on someone else's land. This land was theirs, their bounty, their wealth, their piece of the dream. What we take for granted today was a hard and long fought battle, to be free, to own, and actually live the American dream.

For my Nana; the kitchen was her life, her force of nature, her touch on the world, her grace bestowed upon us.

That same commitment fueled my Nana's Sunday dinners. She would start as early as 4 A.M., preparing a feast before church for the family and any other after-church visitors who would make their way over for some hand-rolled yeast rolls or coconut cake. At a family-style feast, we would gather around the table, have prayer, and enjoy my grandmother's skills: fried chicken, fresh mashed potatoes, string beans with fat back, chitterlings on special occasions, barbecued ribs, potato salad, and candied yams.

But of most desire were the hand-rolled yeast rolls. Freshness was key; she would prepare them early on Sunday morning. Back then, there was no quick-rise yeast, and the dough had to rest for a spell and then be rolled carefully with heavily oiled hands. Each roll would be placed on a sheet pan, side by side, in strict military formation. They would then be covered again and allowed to rest and rise to double their size; then they were ready for baking. She would lay the rolls down by 10, they would make their way into the oven half an hour before church services were to start, and then my Nana would be off getting on her communion Sunday whites or her fancy dress and hat.

A grandchild was always put in charge of the critical responsibility of watching the rolls bake, making sure they were done just right. The perfect color is somewhere between caramel and cocoa brown. On cue, my Nana would arrive back in the kitchen right before leaving for church to butter the rolls while they were still piping hot. We would all be waiting anxiously, and if you were lucky, you could grab a few before leaving for church.

Fresh blackberry preserves, apple jam, strawberry jelly, blueberry jam, would also be set aside as accoutrements.

In 1996, my Papa passed and my Nana a year-and–a-half later. With them went a legacy of ancient times, of commitment, of harvest.

Up until a few years before her death, my Nana, known as the community chef and baker was still doling out these batches of rolls. Many patrons, primarily folks in the direct community and fellow churchgoers, would request her scrumptious rolls, chocolate and coconut cakes, and other delectables, made from only the freshest ingredients. She has passed down some of these time honored processes. My daughter makes a great coconut cake. My chicken stew and blackberry dumplings are to die for. But of most palate admiration were those hand-rolled yeast rolls. My mother, Gloria, resides in my grandparents' former home. She now has become the hand-rolled yeast rolls Madame! I was able to secure this time-honored recipe from her. From her hands to yours.

Hand-Rolled Yeast Rolls

Makes about 3 dozen

½ c. butter, melted
3 c. milk
2 T. salt
½ c. sugar
2 ¼ pkg. Rapid Rise yeast
7 to 8 c. flour
½ c. vegetable oil (for hand rolling)

1. Preheat oven to 350°F.
2. In small saucepan, heat milk to 120 to 130°F. Stir butter into milk.
3. Using electric mixer on low speed, mix three cups flour with salt, sugar, and Rapid Rise yeast. Add milk and butter mixture. Blend using mixer with paddle attachment for one minute. Switch to dough hook attachment. Add remaining flour slowly, until dough forms ball. Rub oil over ball of dough and let rest for 10 minutes.
4. Pinch off small handfuls of dough (about two and one-half by four inches) and shape into balls, rolling under in a circular motion. Place on well greased baking sheets, sides touching. Let rise in warm place until dough doubles.
5. Bake for 18 to 20 minutes or until rolls are between caramel and cocoa brown. Brush with butter. Serve with fresh jam, preserves, and/or Sunday dinner.

SEARCHING FOR *PIÑA* IN HAVANA

Elena Schwolsky-Fitch

In my friend Anita's family, there are seven women named Ana—beginning with her grandmother, descending through her mother Ana Gloria, her *tias* Ana Maria, Ana Margarita, Ana Margot, and Ana Carmen—and finally to her, Anita, the littlest Ana, now a mother herself. She broke the chain when she named her only daughter, my god-daughter, *Rocio*—child of the morning dew.

Anita's family has provided me with a home during a six-month graduate fieldwork project, while I am in Havana in 1996 teaching prevention classes at the AIDS sanitarium on the outskirts of the city. Today we are celebrating Rocio's fifth birthday, and I have spent the morning rounding up ingredients for *ensalada fria*, a cold macaroni salad to serve guests.

Rocio is playing with her friend Diana in the exterior hallway as I trudge up the stairs to the apartment through the sticky August air.

"Elena, Elenita" she calls out to me as I pass. *"Encontraste el jamon?"* Did you find the ham? Even a five-year-old knows how hard this can be. Her father, Jorge, has gone to pick up the candy and cake allowed by the ration card. Anita's mother, Ana Gloria, the second of the Anas, has stayed behind to clean.

Hola, Anita, I'm back. I try to sound cheerful as I put down my bags. I don't want Anita to know I struggled to find the few ingredients, nor to face her disappointment that even my American dollars could not procure *piña*, the essential fresh pineapple.

Encontraste el jamon? Anita comes in from the small patio where she has been hanging up the wash.

"Si, Anita. I bought two nice pieces from the sandwich guy—he even trimmed the fat before weighing. Look at the thick slices."

Sharing the deprivations of my friend's life in Cuba, even in a small way, has given me a new appreciation for things once taken for granted. This morning I arrived at the farmer's market and bought ham, a couple of onions, a green pepper, and two small bulbs of garlic. Then I went to the dollar store, where tourists shop, and bought a jar of green olives, vinegar, and macaroni.

"Anita, este ajo esta seco, es una basura."

Anita's mother is taking things out of bags. The garlic is dried up, she tells me with an exasperated sigh.

"Mami, sientate, sit down and rest," Anita urges. "You're going to make your blood pressure go up again. Don't worry—we'll invent a beautiful salad."

Inventar . . . to invent. How many times a day do I hear Anita use that word now, since things have become so difficult?

"Elena, when do we have the party, when, when?" Rocio bursts through the door as Anita's mother, ignoring her daughter's admonition to rest, puts up water to boil the macaroni. Everything for the party will be cooked in the morning in case there is one of Havana's frequent blackouts later in the day.

"Anita, can you make the *mayonesa?*" Anita's mother calls from the kitchen. They make mayonnaise at home rather than pay $1.89 for a small jar.

"Did you get the eggs from Dianita's mother?" Anita asks. She needs extra eggs for mayonnaise; her neighbor sells them on the black market. Ana Gloria is one of the few Cubans I know who still refuses to buy from black market sellers, but she has relented for Rocio's party. The eggs sit in a bowl, each wrapped in newspaper.

I help Anita assemble the ingredients for *ensalada*. Macaroni, olives, chopped onion, and pepper, a little garlic salvaged from the dry cloves, salt, ham chopped finely, and home-made mayonnaise. A tiny sparrow flies in through the open shutters and steals a piece of ham.

"How I love this kitchen—my little nest among the palm and flamboyant trees!" Anita throws her arms in the air and twirls. An actress in a children's theater group, she is given to dramatic declarations. I know how hard she and Jorge have worked to make this a home and I too love to enter these rooms at the end of a hectic day and feel the peace they have created.

"*Y la piña?*" Anita's mother has reappeared to ask the question I have been dreading all morning.

"No pineapple, Ana Gloria—not in the agro markets, not in the bodegas. I even tried to find canned pineapple in the dollar store. No *piña* anywhere in Havana today."

Anita's mother sits on the couch, her hands chapped and red from washing, her plastic eyeglasses held together with tape. Her shoulders slump and her sigh is heavy with disappointment. *An ensalada fria needs pineapple.*

Ay, Elena, she begins, and I know that I am about to hear about the good old days when her Uncle Tony used to pile the whole family in the back of his truck and take them to the beach at Guardalavaca. Her story will be filled with memories of the flavor and aroma of food—the pig roasted over an open fire, black beans rich with garlic and *vino seco*, yellow rice taken right off the stove. And Tio Tony handing out sandy slices of watermelon and pineapple, the cousins laughing as sweet juice trickles down their arms, and then running, running to the sea.

Ana Gloria's nostalgia is for a time when change was in the air. She hid *guerilleros* in her home during the revolution, and then went to the mountains for the literacy campaign—hiking trails, sleeping in shelters, teaching peasants to read. When she came to Havana, her life was full of undreamed of luxury-her own apartment, a Russian refrigerator awarded for being an outstanding worker, university educations for her daughters, tins of smoked fish and ham on her shelves.

Anita's mother cannot reconcile herself to these years of scarcity and hardship, known as the "special period." She feels betrayed by the whispered offerings of the black market sellers. She feels betrayed by the neighbors whose satellite dish brings TV shows from Miami, by Anita's young co-worker in the theater group who confides his plan to leave for Mexico, by the endless and empty promises of bureaucrats. She feels that betrayal now like hot, acid bile that rises up her throat because there is no pineapple for the salad for her granddaughter's birthday.

I return to the kitchen to help Anita finish the salad. She molds it on a large plate into a clown's face that will amuse Rocio and her friends, with two olives for eyes and strips of red *pimiento* for a mouth.

Jorge will arrive soon, I hope, with the cake. He probably had to wait on a long line—or maybe they ran out of cakes. No matter. Anita will invent this birthday party out of thin air—with blown-up condoms for balloons, with whatever Jorge brings back, with an *ensalada fria* in the shape of a clown.

"Mamita, venga aca." *How Rocio will laugh when she sees what I have done with the salad. Come here and see!*

But Anita's mother doesn't come. She has returned to the patio and is slowly hanging up more wash. She is dreaming, I think, of an island where sweet, ripe pineapples overflow their stands and life does not have to be invented each day.

Cuban *Ensalada Fria*

1 pkg. (16 oz.) elbow macaroni
1 small onion, diced
2 cloves garlic, diced
1 small green pepper, diced
½ lb. ham, finely chopped
¾ c. mayonnaise
1 t. vinegar
Salt and pepper to taste
1 c. fresh pineapple chunks

1. Boil macaroni following package instructions. Drain.
2. In large bowl, combine first five ingredients with mayonnaise, vinegar, salt and pepper, and pineapple chunks. Garnish with pimiento and olives. Chill before serving.

NOT A TONGUE TEMPTER

Sharon Hudgins

Not all foul-tasting foods are the result of a klutz in the kitchen, a cook's overzealous imagination, or a mother's misdirected desire to please (or poison) her family. Sometimes these dishes are just a response to hard times—an attempt to make the most of scarce or inexpensive ingredients, when a mother must feed her family on a meager budget.

When I was a child in the 1950s, our family went through a very difficult period when both of my parents were out of work. Earlier, in better times, they had often bought fresh meat—steaks, roasts, ribs—from a local rancher who belonged to our church. Our small Texas town was the sort of place where my parents left the front door unlocked so the meat man could make deliveries any time of day, even if my folks were away from home.

But when my mother was unemployed because of illness and my father was laid off his job on the railroad, there was little money for luxuries like steaks and roasts. Still, the rancher dropped by our house occasionally, to leave a beef heart, tongue, or liver in our refrigerator, free of charge—offal that none of his customers wanted. I still remember being grossed out the first time I opened the fridge and saw a huge beef tongue lolling on the shelf like some obscene monster that had slipped silently into the kitchen during the night.

But Mother made the most of any meat that showed up. She particularly liked to boil heart and tongue, and then force the cooked meat through a grinder. After that, she'd stir in finely chopped dill pickles and as much mayonnaise as the mixture could hold, to stretch the meat as far as possible. This strong-smelling spread was sandwiched between two pieces of typical American white bread—spongy and tasteless—and served for lunch and dinner, more times than I like to recall. My stomach still turns at the thought of those offal sandwiches—not only because of the taste memory, but also because of the food's association with difficult times. Mother meant well, and we all survived her unsavory sandwiches—but to this day I cringe whenever confronted with any dish containing beef heart or tongue. Mayonnaise and dill pickles are okay.

Offal (Awful) Sandwiches

Serves? Depends on amount of tongue and mayonnaise and number of people you need to feed

1 boiled beef tongue (2 to 3 pounds, skinned and trimmed of all gristle and tough parts), or 1 boiled beef heart (4 to 5 pounds, trimmed of fat and large arteries and veins)

2 to 3 lg. dill pickles, finely chopped
Mayonnaise
Wonder Bread, sliced
Special equipment: Meat grinder and strong stomach.

1. Chop boiled meat into chunks small enough to fit into feed tube of meat grinder fitted with largest grinding disc.
2. Force meat through grinder into large bowl.
3. Stir in chopped pickles and as much mayonnaise as needed to hold mass together. Add more mayonnaise if you need to extend filling.
4. Spread some offal filling (thickly or thinly, depending on your circumstances) on slice of bread. Top with another slice. Do not trim crusts (wasteful!) or cut sandwiches in half for serving. That's way too hoity-toity for this dish.

LOVE'S *YALANCHI*

Rebecca Gopoian

Every Christmas, my parents and I make *yalanchi* (stuffed grape leaves or *sarma*) according to a recipe recited to me by Aunt Lovenia, a woman who has grandmother-status in our family, though she is actually my father's third cousin by marriage. My real Armenian grandmother passed away long ago. Aunt Love is the only one left who knows the old recipe, and her *yalanchi* taste just like my grandma's. Every year, our goal is to make grape leaves that are as good as hers.

For Aunt Love, *yalanchi* is just one of many dishes to make for Christmas. What takes her a few hours takes us an entire day. First, we locate the recipe, scrawled on a scrap of paper. Then we go to the Armenian store for leaves and pine nuts, and the regular supermarket for Carolina rice (the brand of choice for some reason), lemons, olive oil, parsley, and onions, then back to my parents' house in Teaneck, New Jersey, where they can watch my two kids while I chop onions and start cooking.

Since the recipe is barely legible, at some point we call Aunt Love for clarification.

"Really, a whole bottle of olive oil?"

"Yes."

"Did we put allspice in last year?"

"Maybe, but you can skip it."

"How much is 'one mug' of rice?"

"You know, a regular coffee mug."

We don't record these answers because if we did, we would miss next year's annual call.

While the stuffing cools, my dad rinses brine from each leaf. The kids begin their video, and our attention becomes totally focused on the *yalanchi*. Dad and I stuff and roll leaves. Mom arranges them in the pot. We joke about my father's Depression-era frugality and how little rice he puts in each leaf.

We always say, "So this is what it would be like to work in a cigar factory!" We contemplate different methods of stem-snipping and marvel at the range of leaf sizes.

We savor every minute of this laborious yet deeply satisfying process. Since much of our family was killed by the Turks during the Armenian Genocide of 1915 (in which 1 to 1.5 million Armenians were massacred), and the survivors fled to far-flung countries, knowledge of our family history is limited. Making *yalanchi* connects us to a past that would otherwise be lost.

Growing up, I knew that bad things had happened to my grandmother, that she had witnessed family members being killed, that she fled Turkey and followed my grandfather to the United States. Of her four sisters, one was killed, one went to France, and two to Argentina.

Over the years, she saw her French sister a few times, but never those in South America. Then, in her seventies, a recent widow, she decided to visit her one surviving sister in Argentina. How did she feel, traveling by plane for the first time? What did she say to her sister, some 50 years after separation?

I have no way of knowing. But when I visited my relatives in Buenos Aires during college, the *yalanchi* were identical in flavor and consistency to my grandmother's. Clearly, my aunts were following the same recipe, and clearly, this recipe was passed down from my great-grandmother, a woman about whom I know next to nothing, her name penciled uncertainly on the family tree.

When the pot is full, we place an inverted plate on top of the rolls to keep them from popping up while they cook. My mother reminds me to use a plate that's already chipped, and I wonder if this detail has survived generations. When the rolls have cooled, we taste them, but the true test comes on Christmas Eve at Aunt Love's. Her *yalanchi* are perfect: lemony, salty, crunchy yet soft, arranged unassumingly on a platter with *basterma, soujouk, boureg*, and other delicacies. We present our rolls and await her response.

"Very good." (She is kind. We don't call her Aunt Love for nothing.) "Maybe a little more lemon."

We nod, vowing to remember. But even if we master Aunt Love's recipe and follow her advice, our *yalanchi* will never match up. It's not so much that she has magic in her fingers: It's the leaves.

Like my grandmother, Aunt Love grows her own grapes, picks the leaves, freezes or jars them. Fresh leaves are small and tender; store-bought ones are large and tough. Since I can't grow my own leaves, last Christmas Aunt Love mentioned that perhaps she could pick a few for me. This is a little scary. If it happens, I may make grape leaves as good as my grandmother's, or almost as good, or close to almost as good, and if that happens, then what?

I could move on to another dish . . . There's no shortage of gustatory memories to inspire me. But in a way, I'd be disappointed if I could make my grandmother's *yalanchi*. It would lessen the magic of childhood. I'd have to admit I'm no longer the little kid, wowed by her grandmother's cooking. I'm a mother, and my children's connection to Armenian culture is tenuous. They rarely hear the language. They don't attend Armenian school. Our only hope is the food. Unless I learn to make these dishes, and talk to my kids (when they're older) about what happened to my grandparents, their connection to the past will be lost. It's up to me. And the *yalanchi*.

Yalanchi

Makes about 100

7 medium-sized yellow onions, chopped
1 bottle extra virgin olive oil, about 17 oz.
½ c. pine nuts
1 t. salt
1 ½ c. Carolina white rice
½ c. flat leaf parsley, chopped
2 t. dried mint
Dash white pepper
Dash allspice (optional)
1 ½ c. water
6 to 7 T. fresh lemon juice
2 jars grape leaves, 2 lb. each

1. In heavy pot over medium heat, cook onions without oil, stirring frequently until translucent (avoid browning). Add one cup olive oil and cook for one to two minutes. Add pine nuts, salt, mint, parsley, water, white pepper, lemon juice, rice, and allspice, if using. Cover and cook over medium heat about 15 minutes, stirring frequently. Add remaining olive oil. Cover and cook over low heat, stirring frequently, until rice is almost tender but still crunchy.
2. Remove from heat and let mixture cool.

3. Carefully rinse each leaf individually in water to remove brine. Pile on plate. To stuff, lay each leaf on plate and trim stem with sharp knife or scissors. Place about one tablespoon rice mixture in center and roll like a cigar, folding in sides as you go. Then snugly roll top over (where stem was). Rolls should be long and skinny rather than short and fat.

4. Line bottom of large pot with unused leaves (save damaged ones for this purpose). Arrange rolls in pot, end-to-end in concentric circles. Mix one cup water with three to four tablespoons lemon juice and pour over rolls. Invert plate on top of rolls and cover pot with lid. Simmer on low heat for 30 to 40 minutes. Test for consistency. Rice should be cooked through but not mushy.

5. Store in cool place like back porch, but not refrigerator (rice hardens). If you must refrigerate, return rolls to room temperature before serving. Serve with lemon wedges within two days.

END-OF-THE-MONTH FOOD

AnnaLee Wilson

"Filet mignon, medium rare," I say over my shoulder. The waitperson writes down my order. In the background, the Bat Mitzvah girl and her 13-year-old girlfriends in gowns and low-cut socks slide across a polished floor. Some hold each other and dance. Boys roam the room in a pack. In between disco and rap, an entertainer's voice rises in perfect imitation of Roy Orbison singing "Blue Bayou."

Moving around our table, the waitperson recites main course choices to cousins and spouses—filet mignon with balsamic reduction, salmon en croute, or breast of chicken.

"I don't eat meat or poultry, and I just had salmon," Cousin Lena says, shaking her hennaed curls that glisten with silver.

"There's a roasted vegetable platter for vegetarians," our waitperson says.

"Any other fish?"

While the waitperson checks the kitchen, china clatters on china as guests begin to be served. My mouth waters from the smell of other people's meals.

"Our chef can make you filet of sole," she says when she returns.

After Lena agrees, her husband says he really wants filet mignon, but he's given up meat. He orders salmon and a platter of roasted vegetables, too, but without eggplant. Does he think this is a restaurant? At this rate, our table will never get served.

Across the table, my older cousins Jeannie and Myra, both in their early '70s, make comments. They are sisters but they don't look alike. Jeannie smiles with a slight pucker at the side of her mouth. She never shows her teeth, while Myra's face wrinkles inward like a baby when she laughs.

"Remember when we used to eat spaghetti and ketchup?" Jeannie says, sipping her cabernet. "Anytime I'm hungry for something and I don't know what, I make myself a bowl."

"I could never eat it," Lena says.

"It's not good unless you use real butter," says Myra, picking at her greens, sliding radicchio to the rim of her plate.

End-of-the-month food. I hadn't thought of spaghetti and ketchup in years. It's a dish my mother served for dinner when money ran out. I loved it best when it was fresh, before the ketchup soaked into the noodles.

My mother admitted that the first thing she did when my father gave her grocery money from his post-World War II schoolteacher's salary was to splurge on lamb chops, steak, and fresh-killed chickens. It might have been from years of living "on relief," or the loss of both parents before she was 15, but when she got money she had to treat herself. By the third week of the month, with her food allowance dwindling, our family was down to hot dogs and ground meat dishes. She'd have to ask for $10 from Jeannie and Myra's father to get through. Even with the loan, by the last week my mother served end-of-the-month food—vegetables with sour cream, bowties and cottage cheese, or our favorite, thin spaghetti with butter and ketchup. On the fourth Saturday of the month, before my parents left to play cards with friends, my sister and I sat at a yellow Formica-top kitchen table, our feet hooked around the wrought iron chair legs, sucking up ketchup-soaked noodles, letting them dangle from our lips.

The Roy Orbison impersonator takes a break while the Bat Mitzvah guests dine. From the sound of clinking cutlery, everyone in the dining room has been served but us. Then, all at once waiters show up, unfold serving stands, and set down trays holding our orders.

Artfully plated with sauce on top, a pair of inch-thick orbs of beef stare up at me. "Who can eat all this?" I ask.

Lena picks at her fish. She spears some roasted vegetables.

Myra leaves much of her chicken because the meat is dry. I overhear her say she should have ordered filet mignon.

I think of our mothers sharing a tiny flat in Newark, New Jersey, taken in by their sister's husband. There were seven of them in three-and-a-half rooms. Our mothers had no place to go. Orphaned, they were high school dropouts, sharing a bed, looking for jobs, looking for husbands. Eating spaghetti and ketchup for dinner.

Before I can finish the first of my two steaks, disco music starts up. My husband leads me onto the dance floor where he twirls me out then winds me back into the warmth of his body until I get tired and return to the table. Where my main course had been, now sits an elegant presentation of petit fours. I taste them all as waiters pour coffee. The final dessert event arrives with fanfare. Tuxedoed wait staff wheel in draped tables that tower with multilayered cakes and pastries. A fountain gushes with rippling chocolate.

Our bellies full and girded in seat belts on the drive back to New York from the event in Essex County, New Jersey, Lena's husband said, "Chocolate fountains are unsanitary. People stick food in, using their hands."

"And double filet mignons," I say. "I hardly finished one. I hate to see the food thrown out but I wouldn't have the nerve to ask for a doggie bag."

"Why not?" Lena said, sheltering a plastic bag on her lap.

"I could have done without the sauce. You don't need any when the meat is good," my husband said.

"These affairs are so wasteful. Who needs so many choices? Serve two things and be done with it," Lena said.

By five o'clock we're home. I've eaten so much I feel sick. But at nine that evening I find myself hungry for something but I don't know what. Nothing in our bulging freezer appeals to me. The refrigerator holds leftovers of chicken from a takeout dinner, a pork chop, half a yam, a bowlful of noodles. Without hesitation, I reach for the noodles. I'll need butter like the generous chunks my mother worked into hot spaghetti. Using a fork with long tines, she mixed until the yellow melted and every noodle glistened.

The ketchup gives off a tangy aroma when it hits the warm noodles. At first bite, I cough a little from inhaling the vinegary vapor. The taste is sweet and sour, surprisingly good. I eat fast. And it isn't even the end of the month.

End-of-the-Month Spaghetti

Serves 5 to 6

1 lb. thin durum wheat spaghetti
5 to 6 T. salted butter at room temperature, cut in small pieces
1 c. cold or room temperature ketchup, preferably Heinz

1. Boil spaghetti according to package directions.
2. Rinse and drain in colander (I rinse with warm, but not hot, water so noodles don't get cold), then return to cooking pot.

3. Add butter and mix with oversized fork if you have one, making sure butter is thoroughly melted, spaghetti completely coated and glistening.
4. While noodles are still hot, add ketchup and mix.
5. Eat immediately.

JIAO-ZHU (CHINESE DUMPLINGS)

Jashio Pei

My fondest childhood memory comes from when I was six years old living in Beijing, China. I climbed to the top of a huge fig tree and ate the sweet fruits until my tummy ached. While up there, I spied on my aunts doing the laundry on a wooden washing board, hanging pieces on lines, and then filling their mouths with water and spraying the clothes before ironing them. I lived among many aunts and uncles in what was then called Peking while my mom, pregnant with her fourth child, took to bed rest.

My two younger sisters and I spent long afternoons running around the courtyard surrounded by a high stone wall mounted with shards of sharp glass that separated two living structures. When the sun was out, the glass pieces cast fantastic rainbow colors. I would daydream that the fire-spitting dragon would fly over the wall and take me away to some distant fantasyland.

The courtyard was full of vegetable gardens along with chickens and cages of rabbits. I always knew someone special was coming for dinner when chicken feathers flew every which way. Occasionally, we heard tofu and other food vendors hollering outside our red gate and saw our aunts in hot pursuit. Of course, we children eagerly anticipated the arrival of the candy vendors.

I have no recollection of my father then. In fact, when he visited from Japan where he was working, I called him "Uncle." Soon, after my brother was born, we joined our father in Tokyo where we called him Babba. He loved sushi and on occasion brought it home for us to sample. Once we learned it was raw fish, none of us would touch it. Years later, when I was living and working in New York City, I befriended a Japanese woman; she took me to a Japanese restaurant and ordered sushi. For some reason, I didn't want to tell her I had never tried it (after all, I had lived in Japan), so I did. I could have kicked myself for not having eaten sushi in Japan where the real stuff comes from.

While in Japan, Mom got a job with the American army, translating documents from Chinese to English. Although we lived in a modest house, we had a Japanese maid who took care of us while Mom and Babba worked during the day.

Our maid, *Mie-san*, was coached by Mom to prepare traditional Chinese vegetable and meat dishes, always accompanied by white rice. I must have been a growing girl since I can remember having two bowls of rice with every meal. Winter meals always began with piping hot bowls of soup with chicken and various vegetables. Dessert was the freshest fruit in season.

Funny thing is Mom didn't grow up learning how to cook. When she was quite young, her only older brother died and Mom took on his role. She dressed like a boy, shaved her head, and became a scholar. Her father, an engineer schooled in France, wanted her to be ladylike, give up her studies, and learn to cook and sew, but her stepmother insisted that she continue her studies, saying, "She can always learn to cook and sew."

And Mom proved her right by being one of the very few women to attend a university at that time; she earned high grades and only later taught herself how to cook from cookbooks and memories of tastes. I admire my mom for her pioneer spirit and for having been a devoted helpful mate by working most of her life as teacher, translator, typist, banker, and accountant. She is the one I would go to whenever I needed help with my homework. I can still hear her calling "Tsu-fan ler" (Chinese for "dinner is ready") while I was sitting in my room recopying my class notes. That was my favorite time of day. Everyone gathered, stories were told, questions asked and answered.

After dinner, Babba liked to listen to Chinese opera, which to us children sounded like chickens squawking, so we carried on laughing and making fun. Now my children laugh at the Japanese melodies that I like to listen to. My grandchildren perhaps will laugh at those hip-hop songs that my children like.

My fondest memories of my time in Japan are of family gatherings and making *jiao-zhu* (dumplings) on weekends when *Mie-san* enjoyed her days off. Mom prepared the dough, and hand rolling the dumplings into flour balls; one of us four children would chop Chinese cabbage and add ground meat for filling, another would roll out each little ball with a wooden rolling pin, shaping the dumpling wrappers as round as possible. Then everyone would try their hand at putting the dumplings together. This is an art. I prided myself on being the best dumpling maker, three perfectly unified folds on each side, each looking better than the previous one.

My sisters and Mom made fat dumplings, trying to cram in the most filling without bursting the dough open. At times there was a contest to see who could stuff the most into one dumpling. If we ran out of filling, we fought for a turn to create a mystery filling . . . like fruit, nuts, whatever we could imagine–for one lucky person to discover at the dinner table.

While waiting for the big pot of water to boil, Babba made dipping sauce. The sauce itself is quite simple and traditional, but Babba always made the best . . . to this day I'm not sure what extra ingredients he used to make it so fragrant and tasty.

Now that my parents have passed away, whenever my sisters and brother and I visit (we now live in either California or Arizona), we automatically gather in the kitchen and make *jiao-zhu*. We still compare the size, shape, and taste of our dumplings, laugh at broken ones, and each of us hopes to be the one to find that mystery dumpling.

Jiao-Zhu (Chinese Dumplings)

Makes about 50

Wrappers (Can substitute store-bought pot sticker wrappers)

3 c. flour
1 ½ c. warm water

Filling

1 lb. lean ground pork
½ Chinese cabbage, finely chopped (squeeze out liquid)
2 green onions, minced
1 clove garlic, minced
1 T. fresh ginger, minced
2 T. soy sauce
1 T. sesame oil
1 T. rice wine or dry sherry
1 T. cornstarch
Dash black pepper

Sauce

2 T. light soy sauce
1 T. sesame oil
2 T. rice vinegar
1 t. sugar
Chili paste or oil (optional)

Steamed Dumplings

1. In large bowl, combine flour and water with wooden spoon. Knead on lightly floured surface until smooth and form dough into one-inch diameter cylinder.
2. Cut cylinder into three-quarter-inch pieces and flatten each piece with small rolling pin into three-and-one-half-inch diameter circle.
3. Combine all filling mixture into large bowl.
4. Place one tablespoon filling in center of each circle. Fold wrapper over filling, forming half circle. Pinch edges to seal.
5. Fill four-quart saucepan halfway with water. Over medium-high heat, bring to boil.
6. With large spoon, carefully lower about 18 dumplings into boiling water.
7. When water re-boils and dumplings float to top, add one cup of cold water and bring to boil again. Repeat three times.
8. With slotted spoon, scoop out dumplings and serve with sauce.

APPETITES

Heather Wearne

I am just one of the 16 children my mother fed every day. In the memory work I do, I am drawn again and again into my childhood kitchen in Wangaratta, Australia, during the 1960s where the wood stove is always alight, throwing out a warm-body smell of my mother's bread baking. My memory works with leavening effect. The yeast, its heady frothing in flour and oil, suggests to my imagination the rising of our family to its days of so many appetites, the endless feeding of all those hungers.

The kitchen was the center of my mother Audrey's own appetite for order and the busy enterprise of making an impossibly large family a well-fed one. Against the odds. If the history of these things was to be believed, we should have been hungry. My mother's weekly grocery list, written in pencil on a discarded envelope, was the language of our family life. We would wait at home on shopping days and listen for her car. It was a large gray English Humber with red leather seats always marked with small footprints of children. We would hear it roar down the quiet hill into our street, the horn held firmly down by my mother for the whole length of the road. The car would drag up the driveway, heavy with its cargo, as we waited for the moment with ready and hungry hands to whisk out of the car and into the kitchen the huge quantities of food:

a wooden case of oranges,
one of apples,
six pounds bananas;
and in brown-paper bags:
ten pounds of potatoes,
five pounds of carrots,
a bunch of parsnips,
three pounds each of peas and beans;
and in cardboard boxes:
five loaves of bread,
two large jars of Vegemite,
one of peanut butter,
one tin each of apricot jam and orange marmalade,
six pounds of butter,
three dozen eggs,
king-sized boxes of cracker biscuits,
five pounds sugar,
one pound tea,
whole black-green, curling squashes;
and in white butcher's paper parcels of red blood-shiny meat:
five pounds rump steak for grilling,
six pounds blade steak for stews,
a leg of lamb for roast,
lamb loin chops for mid-week,
corned beef for boiling,
lamb chump chops for Irish stew,
lamb shanks and gravy-beef for soups,
and sausages for Saturday lunch in the backyard with tomato sauce and white bread.

For Aud, our large family of eight girls and eight boys was centered on the making of meals. It was the place that defined her daily life and it was where a child's appetite for being part of the world was first discovered: Aud's world.

The hunger of any one of the children to be near our mother was such that, for me at least, standing at the kitchen sink, hands in cold, dirty water, peeling unwashed potatoes, might have been the same as being touched by her. In our busy household, there was never much time for quiet sitting or being held by Aud in gentle arms. She was just too busy, and I cannot remember such a thing happening very often except when a child was sick or a baby being breastfed. So to be the one asked by Aud to roll the pastry, the one who strained the steaming, frothy apples and sprinkled the cinnamon, to be there to watch their transformation into a golden, sugar-dusted dessert, to be praised or thanked, was enough to fill a child with a sense of being well loved.

For a child in this family, kitchen work always held the promise of Aud's recognition. To get a job done as a surprise for her, held the hope of being singled out for notice, for approval, for being a special one among so many. Being with Aud. *Not being with* was awful and the *awful* was often too close for comfort. We also learned when to keep our distance from the kitchen.

My mother's anger on a night when the rooms of the house seemed to shrink and tighten came from a source that was to her many children mysterious. It could feel like a clear slicing blade that cut into the flesh of the day we might just have had, revealing, another surprise, our own child-like bitterness, and surprising us with its vehemence.

Sometimes the recognition came too late:

Larry and I, sitting at the miniature version of the larger kitchen table, a replica in grey laminex and rounded steel legs with black rubber stoppers, miniature laminex-backed, rubber-stoppered chairs; Lal and I giggling over a plate of sausages, potato, peas, tomato sauce. We're there because we are still small enough to fit into the corner near the fridge, because there is no room at the big table, because we like having this, our own miniature table setting where we can tell our own stories. But Lal has his back to Aud. She's at the wood stove, hot with cooking and anger, madly dishing out plate after plate of food. Suddenly, the yell stops everything else, the clunk and clatter of pieces of plate over Lal's head, they're falling onto mine, broken pieces of china-pink and cream flowers, the yellow border petals fall like dropped spears into my pile of mashed potato, skidding across the plate, smothering the peas with bits of china and flattening the potato, pink china flowers scattered in the peas. Lal's face is motley, wet, and fragmenting. His head is covered in small bits of delicate china, and the tears are there but, not knowing which way to go. Aud has gone into her bedroom, banging the kitchen door as a sign that everything, all the noise, all the appetites, it's all too much. We eat our dinner in careful silence.

There are many moods in my memory of Aud's kitchen and I can still see my mother on a very different day and shake my head in wonder. She is playing an long-playing record of Beethoven's settings of three of Goethe's poems; one is *Meerestille* (Calm Sea), and she has propped the collection up against the side of the refrigerator, near the pastry-making bench and she is reading and humming quietly to herself.

These images are as familiar to me as the sound of crying babies and the back door banging on its rubber spring catch. The kitchen of my childhood. My mother. Me and Lal and everyone. All of us there in the kitchen. Being fed. Forever.

Aud's Lamb's Fry Soup

Serves up to 16 with supplements of veggies and rice depending on how many were still at home

There was one odd dish–found in no other home, as far as I know. It was a soup which we called Aud's soup. It was made using a large red lamb's fry (liver!) and was a favorite winter soup for us. Aud used to say that we got more out of a single lamb's fry than the lamb itself ever did. It's very high in protein and cheap to buy–often thrown out by butchers for dog food scrap.

1 lg. lamb's fry (liver)
2 lg. carrots, cut in chunks
2 lg. onions, cut in chunks
2 sticks celery, cut in chunks
1 lg. (600 gram) tin tomatoes
4 rashes (slices) bacon
1 c. white, short-grain uncooked rice
Salt–lots–to taste
Cracked black pepper–to taste

1. Put all ingredients into large (five-liter) stockpot and heat over moderate heat (preferably a slow wood stove) until everything is cooked–about two hours–or until rice and vegetables are soft and soup is rich and thick. Remove lamb's fry (feed it to your dog over the next couple of days).
2. Serve soup hot in large bowls with crusty Italian bread. Add more salt and cracked pepper to taste.

GRANDMOTHER'S GARDEN MEAL

Devon Abbott Mihesuah

My *apokni* (grandmother), Eula, was tall and quiet, with heavily-hooded eyelids she passed on to her descendants. Her great-grandfather was of the

A traditional plated Choctaws meal photographed by the author.

Okla Hannali clan and one of the Choctaws' headmen who felt he had little choice but to sign the infamous removal treaty, also known as the 1830 Treaty with the Choctaws or the Treaty of Dancing Rabbit Creek, in which Choctaws gave up their ancestral lands east of the Mississippi and were forced to march to Oklahoma. Eula's grandfather was a *Nanulhtoka* (light horseman), the sheriff of Sugar Loaf County, *Moshulatubbee* District; her grandmother was Chickasaw, while her great uncle was the son of the Chickasaw chief, Ochantubby.

Nana belonged to the Indian Grandmothers' Club where she lived in Muskogee, Oklahoma, and the Pocahontas Club, whatever that was. According to my childhood interpretation of life, she seemed the opposite of her boisterous Irish, and staunchly Catholic, husband Tom. As I recall, they did not talk much.

I spent a lot of time in my grandmother's kitchen, either eating or sitting at the table, playing with something until food was ready. I never waited long. Nana did not spend hours preparing meals because her dishes, especially those made in summer, were cooked quickly from fresh ingredients straight from her garden. He and Nana could pick, clean, cook, and serve in less than an hour. If she needed a few more onions or some herbs, it was easy just to walk outside and gather more. I never saw her eat red meat, but she did cook chicken, ham, and catfish.

I remember dutifully following Big Tom through his straight rows of *tanchi* (corn), *isito* (squashes), *ahe* (potatoes), and *tobi* (beans). Thick *bissa vpi* (blackberry vines) grew around the fence line. His specialties, okra and tomatoes, became my favorites. Peach trees stood outside the garden perimeter, as did a small toolshed. One morning in early summer, he gently pushed his pitchfork into the soil next to some wilted greenery and pried up a pile of potatoes covered in dirt. To this day I recall my astonishment at learning they grew underground and not on trees. Nana scrubbed those dirty potatoes, along with green pole beans, crooked-neck and zucchini squashes, sweet corn, large red tomatoes, and watermelon, and transformed them into a plate of food that I would prefer over any other. A table laden with fruits and lightly-cooked garden vegetables is indeed unlike any other type of bounty.

These foods, along with *nakishtalali* (catfish), *nita* (bear), *issi* (deer), and *akak chaha* (turkey), are the same foods my ancestors cultivated and hunted. Almost every family made the staple *tamfula*, finely ground and sifted corn, water, and wood ash lye, garnered by pouring cold water over clean wood ashes and collecting the water in a trough. The mixture was boiled from a few hours to all day. When I make *tamfula*, I use a bag of ground corn and cook it in a crock-pot, stirring frequently, so it comes out similar to polenta. Another dish, *banaha*, is similar to Mexican tamales except one might add walnuts, turkey, or ham to the corn mix.

After the Choctaws' traditional Mississippi lands had been taken, the tribal members were forcibly marched to Indian Territory. Burials were left behind as were medicinal plants and *Nanih Waiya*, the site of Choctaws' emergence into the world. It was up to the tribe to reestablish a sense of culture in the new landscape that later became Oklahoma. Luckily, when they migrated west, they found eastern Oklahoma lush and teeming with wildlife.

Fertile soil in Mississippi and Indian Territory allowed Choctaws to cultivate gardens. The woods and streams were full of game animals and fish. The foods my grandparents grew are the same ones that Choctaws historically relied on for survival. Although some tribespeople like to call fry bread (also known as Indian tacos) a "traditional" Indian food, nothing could be further from the truth. Wheat was brought from the Old World, and tribes assigned to reservations learned to fry their flour rations in grease. Before contact, tribes did not drink milk or bake with butter and eggs. Bread was made with corn, camas bulbs, or acorns, and the drink of choice was water. Today, Indians are suffering from unprecedented health problems associated with consuming untraditional, processed foods.

Nana knew that fresh, ripe ingredients provided flavor that can be ruined by adding lard, grease, or too much salt. A light touch of oil in a pan is enough to cook most vegetables and a generous shake of herbs substitutes for sodium. These foods complement each other as a meal and, today, I can't eat a plain baked potato. The spud must be topped with sautéed squashes, green chilies, and tomatoes. If I eat a tomato, I also need a pepper. Green beans must have onions, and key ingredients in my garden salsa are tomatoes, peppers, garlic, and sweet corn. Indeed, I cannot think of another meal that invokes in me such physical and emotional reaction as the garden plate with its mingled, distinctive, earthy flavor.

Eating garden food is greatly symbolic as well as nourishing. At my homes in Flagstaff, Arizona, and now in Kansas, I have tried to emulate Nana's garden and I maintain a Web site devoted to recovering indigenous health. My children understand the importance of eating fresh foods and if I send my daughter Ariana out to pick tomatoes and peppers, I am assured that she eats as many as she puts in the basket.

Growing these same plants as our ancestors and preparing them simply does more than merely honor my grandparents. Raising our own food and using fresh, unprocessed ingredients are not only greatly empowering, they also represent an attempt to mend any disconnect from the land that sustains us. We're making a connection with the past. Eating healthily also means we become aware of where our food comes from, how it is prepared, and by whom.

Vegetable Sauté

Vegetable oil
2 to 3 yellow squash, chopped
2 to 3 zucchini, chopped
2 c. yellow, orange, and red bell peppers, chopped
1 to 2 c. mushrooms, sliced
1 c. green beans
3 lg. tomatoes, sliced
1 lg. sweet onion, chopped
2 to 4 cloves garlic, peeled
Salt, pepper, and herbs such as basil and thyme to taste

1. In large skillet over medium heat, warm oil and vegetables. Sauté for about ten minutes, and then turn.
2. Turn heat to low, cover and simmer until vegetables are tender.
3. Arrange nicely on plate.

These lost worlds are an integral part of us. For better or worse, we need and want to remember. In truth, we can never forget.

3

Restoring Balance

"There's nothing like a good recipe to make you believe things will work out fine in the end," said Avery. "Even the phrase 'Serves four' is hope distilled."[1]
—Anne Michaels, *The Winter Vault*

Almost every recipe is profoundly optimistic. Just follow these directions and the outcome will be pleasing. Inevitably, there are times when the formula doesn't quite deliver, just as there are times when our lives are out of kilter. During these tough stretches, food soothes our transition between where we've been and where we want to be. During mourning, for example, meals taken to the bereaved bring support, love, and healing. Similarly, order is restored to a family when a mother returns to take charge of her kitchen, an admired recipe is converted from weapon to family ownership, and a special cake recipe lost to Katrina's waters is re-constructed. Food signals normalcy and home, and helps get us back on track.

KITCHEN AID: BRINGING FOOD AND FAMILY TOGETHER

Kim Morgan Moss

The moment I heard my sister's voice, I knew something was terribly wrong. "Where have you been?" she asked anxiously, "I've been trying to get you all day!" My younger brother Keith, only 52, had died in his sleep from a heart attack. This happened the night before he was due to move to Connecticut to be near family.

Numbness took hold. My reserved nature has always guarded me from immediate displays of feeling. Emotions must churn through my soul before I can express them. It would take a solid day of cooking and a professional-style KitchenAid mixer to shake my complex reaction loose.

My brother was my mother's favorite, a truth I believed I had accepted. However, during the solitude of the plane ride home, an unexpected flood of emotions came over me—grief, remorse, anger, and jealousy. I forced myself to try to focus on the food for the reception. Cooking is how my family shows its love. It was the way I would show mine.

Before I arrived, Reverend Scott talked with my family about the service. At the end, he suggested gently that they pick up some deli trays of cheeses, meats, and assorted breads for the reception. In unison, my parents and sister responded, "No! We are making all the food; the menu is already planned." Within 24 hours of my brother's death, they had settled this.

A few weeks before he died in January 2009, Keith had a meal my sister served that he really liked. He asked if she would recreate it to celebrate his move to New England. With saddened hearts, this would become the feast in his honor for the memorial service—chicken breasts stuffed with goat cheese and sun dried tomatoes, filet mignon with horseradish sauce, Shrimp Newburg, loaves of Dad's homemade French bread, salad, French green beans, cheesy scalloped potatoes, wild rice and, of course, desserts.

Arriving at my parents' home from Charleston, South Carolina, after midnight gave me only a few hours rest. That morning, fresh coffee, warm hugs, and endless tears awaited me. In no time, we donned aprons and plunged into cooking. Around the big island in the kitchen, we spent the better part of the morning prepping food. Chopping, cutting, and a host of other duties were seasoned with tears and laughter as we shared stories of my brother.

Around midday I said, "The menu is wonderful. But why aren't we making apple pie? It was Keith's favorite; he always asked Mom to make it for his birthday." They agreed that we should add miniature individual rustic apple pies to the already impressive roster of desserts. A few days before, my sister made a carrot cake while my mom baked 50 miniature cheesecakes and 100 chocolate crepes with mousse.

The apple pies were a communal effort. My dad peeled and diced while I made dough. My mom formed the pastry into six-inch rounds, 60 in fact, and then handed them to me for filling. My sister kept an eye on them as they baked, finishing them off with glaze. They turned out lovely—as all the food did—and we couldn't help but sense that my brother was pleased.

I mixed dough in my sister's professional KitchenAid, commenting on how lucky she was to have one. She was surprised I didn't. My sister remembered that Keith had a KitchenAid, packed in storage waiting for his move. She offered it to me. With tears running down my face, I accepted. "I would love it! Do you think it would be okay with him?" With a smile she agreed, "Of course." She knew this would mean a lot to me, especially after I revealed my sadness and remorse for not keeping in touch with my brother. Now he was dead and I was left with a question lingering in my heart: Did Keith know that I loved him? My heart eased when she answered confidently that he did and assured me he would have wanted me to have the mixer.

The day was cold and sunny, the service simple, just as my brother would have wanted. Afterwards, relatives and friends gathered at our house. The food was superb and everyone ate well in Keith's memory.

Families can tug on us, affecting our hearts in both good and hurtful ways. My family is no exception. I regret not being closer to my brother. I thought I would have more time and now there are so many things left unsaid. I have the hope that he is looking down on me, especially when I make his favorite apple pie. Each time I use his KitchenAid, I am given another chance to say, "I love you, Keith."

Rustic Miniature Apple Pies
Makes 12

Pastry

2 c. all-purpose flour
¼ c. sugar
¼ t. kosher salt
2 sticks chilled unsalted butter, cut into ½ T. pieces
¼ to ⅓ c. ice water

Filling

6 to 8 lg. Granny Smith or other tart apples, peeled, cored
2 T. freshly squeezed lemon juice
⅛ c. all-purpose flour
¼ c. sugar
¼ t. salt
1 t. cinnamon
Apple jelly for glazing

Pastry

1. Put flour, sugar, and salt into mixer bowl. Using paddle attachment, blend on low speed for few seconds.
2. Lift up paddle. Add butter and toss mixture with fingers until butter pieces are coated. Turn on mixer and blend on medium-low speed until butter is pea-sized, scraping off paddle with spatula every so often.
3. Add water in slow steady stream until dough begins to gather.
4. Turn out pastry onto well-floured board and form into two discs. Wrap each in plastic and refrigerate at least an hour or overnight.
5. Preheat oven to 425°F. Line baking sheet with parchment paper and set aside.

Filling

1. Cut apples into cubes, toss with remaining filling ingredients, and set aside.
2. Prepare pie shells by dividing one pastry disc into six pieces, then roll each out to about three-inch diameter. Using three-inch cookie or biscuit cutter, cut circles out of each. Set aside scraps. Roll each circle out to about six inches, being careful to keep round shape.
3. Spoon a few tablespoons apple mixture into center of each circle, leaving about one-and-half to two-inch border. Pull up borders, folding over filling. Carefully transfer to baking sheet and repeat process with remaining disc of dough, scraps too, if necessary. Bake for about 20 to 22 minutes, or until crust is golden.
4. In small saucepan, heat and melt apple jelly. While pies are still warm, brush edges of pastry and apples with jelly.
5. Remove parchment with pastries from pan, sliding off sheet to rack to cool. Serve warm or cold.

The pies keep well for a few days if they last that long!

JUST DESSERT

Sharon Hudgins

Mother was reluctant to relinquish her homemaker role to a stranger. Chalk it up to 1950s middle-class guilt. But she was teaching full time at an elementary school in Denison, Texas, had a husband who worked erratic shifts on the railroad, lived in a dusty house, and had two little girls to feed every day. She needed help.

Enter Mrs. McCoy (the name has been changed to protect the guilty)—our first, and last, housekeeper-cook. She was a well-meaning woman, a widow in her sixties, tiny in stature, with brightly dyed jet-black hair and a host of allergies. Fortunately for us, the only meal she had to cook every day was lunch, when our family of four came home to eat. I don't think we could have survived more than that.

She was the worst cook I have ever encountered. That woman could ruin instant potatoes—and very often did. She made them the consistency of cream gravy so they kept running off the plate and had the taste of Pablum. Her signature meat dish was unseasoned ground beef swimming in something that looked suspiciously like library paste. I think it was supposed to be a casserole.

Mrs. McCoy's favorite dessert was chocolate pudding—the kind where you put two cups of milk into a saucepan, add the contents of a box of pudding mix, cook until the mixture begins to thicken, and then serve either warm or chilled. Easy, yes? Not for Mrs. McCoy. No matter how many times my mother explained this simple set of directions, she kept on cooking the chocolate pudding her own way.

So we continued to face the same fiasco for dessert each day. Mrs. McCoy really liked making chocolate pudding from a mix. And she insisted on sneaking in two whole eggs sometime during the cooking process. The result was a gunky, liver-colored mass that stuck to your teeth, hung onto the roof of your mouth, and was reluctant to travel any farther down your gullet.

One day her attempt to dress up this dessert proved to be the last straw. After another ground-beef-casserole lunch, Mrs. McCoy proudly presented us with her surprise: chocolate pudding crowned with meringue. She had smoothed the prepared pudding into a shallow baking dish and whipped (or so she thought) some egg whites to spread on top for meringue. The poorly beaten egg whites, floating on the egg-infested pudding mix, had then gone into a not-very-hot oven to "bake."

When this affront to civilization was placed on the table, we just stared at it, not knowing what to do next. As slimy, undercooked egg whites ran out under the slightly cooked meringue, the library paste began churning in our stomachs. My father finally reached out and touched the quivering substance to see if it were real. Then he pulled the entire pudding out of the pan in one piece, since the eggs had solidified it into a cohesive block. He sat there with a look of astonishment on his face, holding the rubbery mass in both hands as uncooked egg whites dripped off the sides.

I can't recall what happened next, but I do remember that Mrs. McCoy departed from our household soon after that meal. She left for California to marry someone she'd met through a lonely-hearts correspondence club. The poor man had no idea what he was getting into.

Mother returned to the kitchen in addition to keeping up her classroom commitments. She was a good cook who especially enjoyed baking, from batches of cookies to pans of yeasty cinnamon rolls. Her Chocolate Pudding Cake was one of those simple recipes so popular in the 1950s—a rich, gooey, calorie-laden comfort food, easy and quick to make after a long day at school. Today, one taste of it instantly evokes childhood memories of warm kitchens on cold days, with the aroma of chocolate filling our little frame house in the suburbs.

Chocolate Pudding Cake

Serves 6 to 8

 This rich, pecan-studded white cake makes its own chocolate sauce while it bakes. The recipe and its title come from my mother's handwritten recipe cards—although it should more accurately be called Chocolate-Sauce Pecan Cake. Don't be tempted to mess with the recipe by stirring the toppings into the batter before popping the pan into the oven! But do be sure to use the correct size (eight-inch-square) metal baking pan, which is crucial to the success of this dessert.

Cake

¼ c. (4 T.) cold unsalted butter
¾ c. sugar
1 ¼ c. all-purpose flour
2 ½ t. baking powder
½ t. salt
¾ c. milk
1 t. vanilla extract
¾ c. pecans, chopped

Topping

1 c. brown sugar, firmly packed
¼ c. unsweetened cocoa
¼ t. salt
1 c. boiling water

1. Preheat oven to 375°F. Butter eight-inch square pan. Put small kettle of water on to boil.
2. Cut cold butter into small pieces. In large bowl of electric mixer on medium speed, beat butter and sugar together until completely combined and no lumps of butter remain.
3. In small bowl, sift flour, baking powder, and salt together. Measure out milk in glass measuring cup and stir in vanilla extract.
4. Add flour mixture alternately with milk to butter-sugar mixture, about a quarter cup at a time, stirring well after each addition. Stir in chopped nuts. Spread batter evenly in prepared baking pan.
5. Stir together brown sugar, cocoa, and salt until well mixed, breaking up lumps. Sprinkle topping in even layer over batter. Carefully pour boiling water over cocoa/brown sugar mixture, completely covering topping. *Do not stir* water into other ingredients.
6. Put pan into oven immediately and bake on middle rack for 40 minutes. Cake batter will rise to top and float on chocolate sauce underneath.
7. Let pudding cake cool in pan on wire rack for 10 to 15 minutes. Spoon cake onto individual dessert plates or into shallow dessert bowls, adding some chocolate sauce over each portion. Serve warm or at room temperature. (Cover and refrigerate leftovers.)

GRANDMA SADIE'S *RUGELACH*

Anita Gallers

My grandmother, Sadie Gallers, made the best *rugelach*. I know what you're thinking: "No, *my* grandmother made the best *rugelach*." Or maybe it was your aunt, or your best friend's mother. I assure you that you are mistaken. Try the recipe and you'll see.

Grandma was a proud lady. To look at her, you might think she was a tiny old woman, but talk to her and you'd quickly realize she was a tough old broad. She was an old-school, will-of-iron, wit-of-steel Jewish mother from the Bronx. And other than her children, grandchildren, and great-grandchildren, these cookies were one of the things of which she was most proud because the *rugelach* were one of the few things she could unequivocally claim as *hers*. Not the degree she always regretted not getting, perhaps, but people loved them, and through them, Grandma achieved a kind of fame. These cookies were her invention, her creation, her achievement.

And Grandma wasn't wrong: any batch of pastries that good is an accomplishment. But as much as Grandma wanted to share her cookies, she exacted a price. You had to praise the *rugelach* to high heaven, first of all. If you neglected this tithe of flattery, Grandma wouldn't hesitate to extract it. The harder part was listening to her anecdotes—some recent, some of unknown age—about who else had eaten and loved her *rugelach*, who had asked her to make them specially for his visit, who had shared her batch at work to universal raves. It always made me sad that her desperation for acknowledgment typified the ways she managed to irritate, even alienate, those she most desired to be close to.

For example, when I asked for the recipe, she was gratified, yet her overbearing manner colored the bond we were forming. We had repeated telephone conversations about it while I was living in New Haven, Connecticut; since it wasn't a formal, written recipe, she called me back multiple times to clarify one piece or another; she also called several times to find out if I had made them yet, and when I finally did, we had a more extensive debriefing about whether I had found it difficult, and how the cookies turned out.

Alas, the recipe that Grandma and I bonded over was later a source of tension. Unfortunately for my father, no woman was ever good enough for him in his mother's eyes. With each of his three marriages, Grandma worked successively harder to compete with, denigrate, and disaffect his wives. Dad's current wife, Chandra, is easily one of the warmest people I know. Her particular respect for parents and elders led her to cater to her mother-in-law; she was also a frequent peacemaker between Dad and Grandma, whose relationship was both close and fraught. But Grandma, ever jealous and mistrustful, could not see what a boon her daughter-in-law was to her son or to herself. As Grandma became increasingly suspicious of Chandra and picked fights with her, one of her weapons was the *rugelach* recipe.

In happier times, when Grandma appreciated Chandra's attentions, she had offered to show Chandra how to make *rugelach*, and Chandra, who likes both cooking and doing the little things that mean so much to other people, had wanted to learn. But now, Grandma vowed never to give Chandra the recipe, swearing she would take it to her grave. When she was reminded that she had already given it to me, she said that she regretted it. Dad, Chandra, and I laughed about this. But Grandma was dead serious. From her perspective, I think, she was trying to maintain control of her precious intellectual property, to keep her artistic process away from the unworthy—and in so doing, inflict harm. My possession of the recipe was a chink in her armor: the recipe was no longer wholly hers to give or withhold.

I found myself in the awkward position of wanting to share it with Chandra, which seemed the least I could do for someone who deserved so much better, and, on the other hand, wanting to respect Grandma's wishes. The compromise I struck with myself was to respect Grandma's wishes as long as she lived, and to give Chandra the recipe after Grandma died. Indeed, some weeks after Grandma's passing, I sent it to Dad.

I thought long and hard about whether it was appropriate for me to publish the recipe. I have decided I want to help Grandma take her recipe beyond the grave, spread her acclaim—to help, if I can, heal her loneliness, isolation, and desperation for recognition, by bonding her memory and spirit to every person who makes her signature cookies. So please use and share it. And when you share the cookies, make sure to say that they're Grandma Sadie's.

Rugelach

Makes about 4 dozen

The main body of the recipe reads just how Grandma told me to make them. She used no measurements for the filling, so I have done my best to estimate. My editorial remarks and additions are in parentheses.

½ lb. margarine
½ lb. cream cheese
2 c. flour
1 T. vanilla
10 oz. jar jam (Grandma used strawberry)
Sugar and cinnamon, combined (I'd say 3 T. sugar to 2 t. cinnamon)
1 ½ c. chopped walnuts
1 ½ to 2 c. yellow raisins, soaked in warm water for 15 minutes and drained

1. Preheat oven to 400°F.
2. Knead margarine, cream cheese, flour, and vanilla into ball. (I sometimes use standing mixer for this.) Wrap in foil (or waxed paper) and refrigerate at least two to three hours.
3. Divide dough into five pieces. Roll out each piece into a rectangle. (Dough is sticky. Make sure to flour both your rolling surface and your rolling pin well.) Spread on an even layer of jam. (I spread jam over the bottom two-thirds of the rectangle, leaving space for the final roll.) Sprinkle cinnamon and sugar mixture over jam. Then sprinkle chopped walnuts and raisins. (I have also used other nut and fruit combinations, such as almonds and chopped dried apricots—particularly good with blueberry jam.)
4. Roll each dough coated piece lengthwise. Place on foil-lined cookie sheet. Slice crosswise. (I slice on the cutting board, then transfer them with a spatula to a nonstick cookie sheet. My experience is that the inevitable

baked-on jam overflow comes off a quality cookie sheet easily enough so that you don't really need foil, but I like to use a silicone liner to make the cleanup ultra-easy.)

5. Bake for about 45 minutes, until edges start to brown. Cool slightly on sheet and then on wire racks.

DEATH *HELVA*

Tijen Inaltong

"I really hope tomorrow comes soon," my grandma said in a childlike voice, lying in her bed. "I missed having breakfast."

I smiled. She had just eaten breakfast and the next morning was only a few hours away.

"I want toasted bread, jam, and cream," she whispered. Knowing that I would oppose her, she added, "please." We knew these were her last days. So why refuse? Sugar was not good for her cancer but she was dying. Was it worth taking her unique enjoyment away?

My grandma died five years ago. We didn't have a blood relationship. She was my grandfather's second wife, but we accepted her as our grandma and enjoyed the *gözleme* she made occasionally, when we gathered in our or any of my aunts' houses. I remember the smell of the crunchy, tasty pastry she began making early in the morning, while the rest of us slept. It is easy to prepare the dough. All that is needed is flour and water. The preparation requires some resting time; that's why she got up so early. She would divide the dough into several rounds, each smaller than a fist. When the time came to roll them, she would clean the round kitchen table where I also studied, sprinkle it with flour, and roll the first dough into a thin round. She would then sprinkle it with oil, usually a mixture of melted butter and sunflower or corn oil.

Like puff pastry, the dough needs to be folded like an envelope, rolled again, a bit more oil, one more rolling . . . This goes on until the dough becomes quite oily, which gives it crustiness, similar to a croissant. When the time came (she always knew when), she would roll each one with her palms to make a long tube, then twist them into spirals to make circles, roll a bit to make each flat, and fry them in a little butter-oil. I would usually wake at this point in the ritual, and go directly to the kitchen to watch her roll out each piece, fry them one by one. Sometimes either my mom or one of my aunts would help with the frying while we kids set the table. We would, of course, brew the tea, and then cut feta cheese, fill bowls with olives and a variety of jams (sour cherry, strawberry, apricot, plum) while the pastries were frying. We also needed paper napkins since we would eat the pastries with our hands (that's the best way to enjoy a *gözleme,* also known as *katmer*). The frying process would continue while we were eating because *gözleme* taste best warm.

My grandmother's *gözleme* was the best I have ever tasted. I also loved the doughnut-like sweet pastry, *çay lokması,* she sometimes made. I had never acquired the directions, although I feel certain I can make it because I watched carefully so many times. Luckily, one of my aunts wrote down the recipe, and recently gave me a copy.

My grandma lost consciousness a few days later. She needed to be fed through a tube. It was heartbreaking. She had been a beautiful woman. She never stopped dyeing her hair.

The day my grandmother died, my mom and aunts prepared *helva* in her memory. It is a custom in Turkey when someone dies to make this sweet and distribute it to neighbors and friends. My mom says it is always good to have many people at home to help make the confection. It is believed that stirring the "death *helva*" is meritorious, so many women volunteer and say prayers while they work.

The ingredients of *helva* are in every kitchen cupboard in Turkey: wheat flour, butter (although many people use margarine), sugar, and water. While pine nuts and milk improve the taste, their use is optional. Sometimes semolina is used instead of flour. Although it is easier to make semolina *helva,* flour is queen. Regardless of the ingredients, making *helva* is labor-intensive. The longer one fries the flour, the tastier it becomes. As soon as it turns pink, pine nuts are added and the stirring continues. When the nuts are browned, it is time to add the boiled water, mixed with sugar. Once the *helva* is cooked, it is shaped and plated to serve.

Using a wooden spoon, the *helva* is shaped into oval balls, and then arranged on small plates covered with paper towels. It is the duty of the girls in the family to distribute them. We usually ask recipients to remove the *helva* from the plates right away; otherwise, they will be obliged to return them to us filled with food! Customarily, neighbors and friends bring food after the funeral. When there is sadness, it is shared through food. They bring whatever they can cook, the same as we will do when they have a death in their house. Don't we all need each other at those times?

In Turkey, at the home of the deceased, nothing is cooked for at least a week. Friends and neighbors feed the family during the mourning period. They may bring a homemade soup; *börek,* a pastry that is either hand-rolled or made with ready-made phyllo pastry filled with cheese, meat, or vegetables—it may be eaten for breakfast as well as dinner; sweets, cakes, or pastries to be served to guests who visit to offer condolences. Tea that accompanies pastries usually brews on the stove all day long, ready for each new arrival.

Yes, *helva* is what Mom and my aunts made when my grandmother died. They had friends to share the responsibilities. And their friends had them to bring food when they lost loved ones, to bring love and hugs or shoulders on which to cry. When someone knocks on your door with a plate of *helva*, you know the reason. It's to share a happy occasion, a sad one, or as a remembrance. Taking the plate of *helva* symbolizes the sharing of feeling, happy or sad, a sense of community.

There are many reasons for stirring *helva* and there are times we prepare it for no reason at all, just for the sake of having sweets. But believe me, sharing it with loved ones extends the meaning. It may be just a reminder of how our neighbors and friends are there for us or just to say we need them in good times and bad.

Un Helvasi (Flour *Helva*)

Serves 6 to 8

Not only is this shared when someone dies, it is also served on the anniversary of the death.

Dough

1 ½ c. white or whole wheat flour
8 T. (1 stick) butter, unsalted
2 to 3 T. pine nuts

Syrup

2 c. water
1 ¼ c. sugar

1. In heavy frying pan over very low heat, melt butter, add flour, and stir constantly with wooden spoon at least 30 minutes until flour turns nutty brown and gives off toasted aroma. Add pine nuts. Keep stirring until they turn deeper brown. Do not allow to burn.
2. Meanwhile, in medium saucepan, heat water and sugar over moderate heat until sugar dissolves and mixture reaches consistency of thin syrup. When

mixture boils, add syrup to dry mixture, stirring rapidly (and carefully as mixture is quite hot) until thickened and water evaporates.

3. Shape immediately, using spoon to scoop dough and press on side of pot to create ovals and place on plates. *Helva* may be eaten warm or at room temperature depending on personal preference. Both are tasty.

OMA SPRINGER'S CHRISTMAS CARP

Alexandra Springer

Christmas has always been my favorite holiday. Then, and only then, my entire family of 17 would gather at my uncle's house in Germany. Not having any brothers and sisters, I enjoyed this holiday enormously for it made me realize that I was part of a great big family.

The main dishes were prepared by my grandmother at her small house, not much bigger than 450 square feet. My grandparents had lived through World War II where they experienced extreme hardship, the utmost being the death of their youngest son (my uncle and father's younger brother) of starvation/malnutrition at age two. My grandparents left Germany in the 1930s due to high unemployment and moved to France where they experienced similar labor surpluses only a couple years later. They then moved to Czechoslovakia where they resided for a few years before work opportunities withered and they were forced to move again. This time they went back to Germany where they would stay until they both passed away.

During this time of the Great Depression, my grandparents had to leave everything behind each time they moved. I assume this is the reason that I never heard them complain about their house with only a living room, small bedroom, tiny kitchen, and very tiny bathroom.

Today, I live in a small apartment in which kitchen and living room are one, and every time I try to justify why I cannot make elaborate meals, I stop and think about all that my grandma prepared every day. How small is "small"? When she stood in front of her stove and turned around, she was immediately up against her working/dining table (both table and stove were placed against opposite walls.) Still, my grandma managed to bake the most sophisticated apple strudel, *kolatchki* (pastry filled with jelly) and *striezel* (plaited bun) and prepared the greatest meals without ever expressing any inconvenience.

Christmas dinner entailed the same dishes every year: roast goose, red cabbage, *bömischer kloss* (a very large dumpling sliced with a thread of yarn), lentils (which all the children hated, but were told would bring good luck for the coming year), *kuba* (a dish made of pearl barley, garlic, salt and pepper, and porcini mushrooms my grandmother collected during August and September, then hung to dry in the sun), potato salad, herring salad (prepared on special request for my grandfather), fish soup, and fried carp. While many of the dishes had a special purpose, it was the carp that had most significance.

Every year two or three days before Christmas Eve, my grandfather, and in later years my uncle or dad, picked up two or three preordered fresh (read alive) carp. Each would normally weigh over four pounds. They would then bring the carp to my grandmother's house where a bathtub full of fresh water was waiting. The fish would swim until Christmas Day. During this time almost every family member would have stopped by, huddling over the bathtub, reaffirming what "great specimen of carp" these were, while we kids would try to pet them.

On Christmas Day, my grandma would prepare the carp by first hitting them on the heads with a meat hammer, cutting off the heads (which would become stock for the soup we would eat later), and de-scaling the fish with the back of a large cutting knife. She then cut them into cutlets, fried, and served them.

The role of the carp in Christmas did not end there, however. After dinner we opened gifts that had mysteriously appeared under the tree while we were eating. Of course, officially *Das Christkind* came during dinner and placed the presents, but we always seemed to miss his arrival. After opening presents, my grandma would give every family member "a little package" no bigger than a quarter. It contained a few fish scales wrapped in a little piece of white paper towel. She never made a big deal about it when she handed us the "little packages" and would do it in such an unobtrusive way, such as walking by and slipping it into your hand saying, "Put it in your wallet so you will never run out of change in the coming year."

Neither my uncle nor Dad remembers when my grandmother started this tradition. They simply told me that "it was always done this way." I do not remember when I received my first "little package," but like every other family member, I placed it in the coin part of my wallet and left it there until the following Christmas when everyone received a replacement.

By the time Christmas came around again, the old package was pretty beat up. Little pieces of paper towel and dried fish scales were scattered among the change. I am confident that no one particularly enjoyed this and I am not certain how many of my family members really believed that this "little package" would ensure that they would not run out of money. But I can confirm that not one dared remove it before receiving the new one.

My grandmother passed away in 2003 and with her, all the traditions connected to the carp. While I have described this practice to a few people over the years it was not until I actually wrote down this story that I realized how much I miss seeing this "little white package" every time I open my wallet.

Christmas Carp

This recipe is as close as it gets to accurate volume measurements. It was impossible to get any recipe from my grandma that had actual kitchen measurements. Every time I watched her prepare a dish and I would try to write down the recipe, I only ended up with the ingredients and notes such as "a handful of flour," "a little salt," "you'll see if more eggs are needed . . .," and "add more milk if necessary." The same information I received when I asked how long and at what temperature something had to be cooked. She always replied "you'll see when it's ready" and the temperature was either "low," "middle," or "hot."

1 carp, about 2 lb.
2 to 4 c. flour
6 to 8 eggs
Salt and pepper
2 to 3 c. breadcrumbs, homemade
Vegetable oil

1. Kill, de-scale, and clean carp. Remove head and save for stock. Cut carp in large, vertical pieces. Dip first in flour, then egg mixture seasoned with (plenty of) salt and pepper. Coat pieces with breadcrumbs.
2. Heat oil in skillet over medium heat until drop of water dripped in sizzles. Fry pieces slowly until golden brown.
3. Remove with spatula and plate pieces.

AFTER KATRINA

Amy Cyrex Sins

My first inkling that Katrina was a storm like no other came after I had evacuated to Houston. I watched in horror on national television as the levee on the 17th Street Canal (only ten houses from our own) broke, sending tons of water and debris down our street. This break, which wouldn't have happened if the levees had been properly engineered, caused the major flooding throughout New Orleans. I could see the roofline of our house on the screen, and I could tell that it was flooded but not how deep. Many homes were destroyed beyond re-building.

When disaster struck, it didn't surprise me that the people of New Orleans yearned more than ever for that taste of home, dishes that reminded them of family and normalcy. Centuries of tradition have lead to distinctive Creole and Cajun dishes, as well as deep-rooted southern foodways. Many people don't realize how important food is to the people of Louisiana; it is truly a way of life. That's why even though our home was under water, and coated with mold and mud, I mourned the loss of my recipe collection.

Food defines important moments for me. I loved my wedding cake, totally non-traditional—white chocolate filled with raspberry. Our guests still talk about it over five years later. Then there's Doberge Cake, light, fluffy, and moist, a traditional New Orleans treat piled eight layers high, filled with chocolate custard and slathered with chocolate ganache. My mother-in-law, Janet Sins, always made it for my husband's birthday. For my own, she made a special chicken recipe, known as Birthday Chicken that she prepared only for my day because it was so much work—layers of chicken, pounded flat and covered with parmesan cheese, green onions, and mushroom-wine sauce. And I wouldn't stop with family, there's so much more—jambalaya at the church fair, fried fish at the grocery during Lent, beignets when your maw maw takes you to Morning Call. Happy, Sad, Momentous, and Every Day, food marks life events.

Hurricane Katrina didn't change that for me; it only made it more poignant. Many days later, my husband and I returned to survey the damage. When we got to our street, we were in shock. Mud, trees, and other unidentifiable objects were piled high; mounds of dirt and debris stacked up as tall as twenty feet. The only way we could access our house was by four-wheel all-terrain vehicle. Incredibly, we found a house from three blocks away sitting in our driveway.

Opening the front door of our house was impossible. Wearing masks, rubber boots, and gloves, we slipped and slid along, climbing mounds to what had been our backyard. Then it hit us—the SMELL. I can only compare it to a port-a-potty on the last day of Mardi Gras. It will stay with me forever.

When we entered through our blown down back doors, we found a six-inch layer of black slimy mud covering the entire first floor. Mold was growing out of control like a fuzzy marine animal climbing our walls.

Nothing was as it had been. Katrina had a capricious sense of humor. A bottle of Sprite had migrated from the kitchen to the living room and was holding up a batch of encyclopedias. My canister of sugar had been transported to the top shelf of our entertainment center as if for decoration.

Only our china cabinet hadn't moved—the one my husband always said contained too much unnecessary stuff. Somewhere in the murky mud that surrounded it were my precious, but unrecognizable, cookbooks.

Everything considered, we were, of course, very lucky. We didn't lose people. My husband had saved our cats, Frank and Dean, named for Frank Sinatra and Dean Martin, and many of our photos. What was left was "stuff" not without emotional attachment, but replicable. Well, mostly replicable.

Lost forever were the family recipes I had collected and cherished. Whenever I had attended a great party or had a fabulous meal at a restaurant or someone brought an excellent dish to a potluck, I would ask for the recipe. There had been food clippings from newspapers (everyone from the *Times Picayune* since I had moved to New Orleans), magazine articles, recipes from my mother-in-law, and a few trial-and-error formulas when my friends and I would try to "touch up" recipes from cookbooks.

Most of my favorites came from my mother-in-law who lived only a few miles away. Her home was also flooded and her collection destroyed. She salvaged a few handwritten cards which she stored in ziplock bags. Many were the only remembrances she had in the handwriting of female relatives no longer alive. With her help, and the entire community's, I'm trying to reassemble my recipes; it takes many false attempts and adjustments to recapture the exact flavor and texture.

Take Doberge Cake, for example. On my husband's first birthday after Katrina, the torch passed from my mother-in-law to me to make this all-important confection. Fortunately, I had two cake pans in the galley kitchen of our temporary French Quarter apartment, and I set to work. The cake was the easy part, but re-constructing the family recipe for ganache proved elusive. Janet and I can only remember a few ingredients–corn syrup, chocolate bits, and cream. I've made it several times but my husband George always tells me it's not quite right. "Sorry babe, that's just not the same."

After gaining 15 pounds trying to duplicate Doberge Cake, as well as other pre-Katrina classics, I'm reserving the confection for special occasions! For now, this re-constructed recipe will have to do.

Doberge Cake

Serves 12

The inexperienced baker tends to produce a leaning tower, but with much practice, a perfect upright cake will be possible.

Cake

2 Betty Crocker Butter Yellow Cake mixes

1. Follow package directions to make four layers.
2. Cool layers on wire racks.
3. Using saw-toothed knife, cut each layer horizontally into two. This is easiest if you use toothpicks to mark the halfway point where you intend to cut. You will then have eight layers in all.

Filling

1 c. sugar
½ c. flour
3 c. milk
4 eggs
1 ½ t. vanilla extract
3 ½ oz. Lindt dark chocolate bar, chopped

1. In medium saucepan over medium-high heat, quickly combine sugar and flour. Gradually stir in milk and chopped chocolate. Heat until thick and bubbly and chocolate is completely melted. Reduce heat to very low and cook two minutes more. Remove from heat.
2. Separate eggs into two small bowls. Gradually add cup of filling to yolks to temper them and prevent scrambling. Then add yolk mixture to saucepan. Return to heat and bring to gentle boil. Stir in butter and vanilla.
3. Cover with cling wrap touching mixture to prevent skin from forming and chill in refrigerator one hour.

Ganache

1 lb. (1 box) confectioners' sugar
2 T. light corn syrup
⅓ c. water
2 squares (2 oz.) unsweetened chocolate, melted
½ t. vanilla extract

1. Sift confectioner's sugar into large bowl.
2. In small saucepan, mix corn syrup and water and bring to boil.
3. Remove from heat and pour into confectioners' sugar.
4. Add melted chocolate and vanilla extract and combine all ingredients.

Ganache will be fairly thin, but not runny.

Assembling Cake

1. Smooth filling between layers of cake and stack them. You may hold the confection together with a wooden skewer.
2. Pour ganache over top to cover entire cake. Cool in refrigerator for two hours before serving. Icing will harden. Enjoy!

No matter how dark things may seem at some points of our lives, food helps us regain our bearings and work through our feelings so we can emerge with greater equanimity and renewed harmony.

4

Life Lessons

Stories transform our experiences into ways of knowing—about ourselves as women and about ourselves as women looking at the world.[1]
—Bettina Aptheker, Tapestries of Life: Women's Work, Women's Consciousness, and the Meaning of Daily Existence

Some tales of iconic dishes embody valuable life knowledge, as well as kitchen wisdom. In one narrative, food works as a healer in a most mysterious way. One author discovers that baking special cakes for her children, like her mother did, is not a symbol of oppression but a profound expression of mother love. Through a grandmother, a woman learns that anticipation—the looking forward to an experience—enhances rather than detracts from its pleasure. Another story involves lessons about blending disparate members into a true family, constantly massaging them into a whole. There is really no end to the life lessons learned from storied dishes.

NAEMAT ALLAH

Ashley Makar

On her first night in the United States, my Aunt Elene pulled a bag of dry lentils out of her suitcase, poured a cup on the kitchen table, and started moving them around with her tiny, crooked index finger. She came to visit us from Alexandria, Egypt, to Alabama for two months every summer. She was separating discolored lentils from bright orange ones that she would simmer into a yellow mush overnight. By morning, the refrigerator was full of food from Alexandria—jars of pickled lemons, cartons of soft, white cheese, and *helawa*, a sweet sesame paste. Every burner of the stove was occupied: chunks of meat boiling into beef stock, loose tea brewing in a saucepan, cauliflower frying in a skillet.

When I saw Elene hunching over a barely bubbling milky substance, stirring continuously, I thought she was making pudding. But she added salt, not sugar, and white pepper, not vanilla. I stood beside her, watching—stir by stir, the slow-rolling liquid thickened, as imperceptibly as twilight became dark. I witnessed the miracle moment it turned, as if by a singular stroke of the spoon, into béchamel. She then removed the saucepan, turned up the heat, and put on a pot of water to boil for noodles. On another burner, she started frying the onion she'd cut fine as pulp—a paring knife in her right hand, the onion in her left, suspended over a bowl. Once the onion turned from white to clear yellow, she added ground beef, using a tablespoon to break up the meat and spread it evenly over the heat. Once the meat was browned, she drained the noodles and mixed them with half of the cooling béchamel. I realized she was making what I then called Egyptian macaroni, which she assembled like lasagna: a layer of noodles, a layer of meat, until she brushed the béchamel on top with beaten egg and put it in the oven.

After Elene finished layering, she would move the spoon around the saucepan, scraping up all the remaining béchamel, and bring it to my mouth.

"Eat," she would say, one of the few English words she'd picked up. "*Yalla*," (Arabic for "come on") *diy naemat allah!*"

"She believes it is a sin to throw food away," my father explained in exasperated English, "to waste what God provides."

Naemat allah must be why Elene would stand over the sink sucking every bit of fish from the bones we would leave, far from clean, on our plates. And why, when my father was recovering from a kidney transplant, she lived on saltines and black coffee he would leave on his hospital tray. I would bring her fast-food hamburgers, and she would put her hand over her heart to decline, saying, "*Je fais la Carême.*"

My father interpreted again for me: "She believes her sacrifice will help make me well."

I didn't know then if *carême* was Arabic or French. (Elene spoke both to me, sometimes in the same phrase.) I just knew it meant she wouldn't be eating the macaroni béchamel she'd spent all day making for us, or having her staple of hard-boiled egg and feta cheese sandwiches, or even milk in her tea. When Elene said "*Je fais la Carême*," she would be living mostly on lentils—for weeks at a time. She wouldn't really eat until sundown on Good Friday.

Later, I learned that "*faire la Carême*" means "to fast;" literally, "to make Lent." And *carême* is related to the Arabic root for "offering"—*qurban*—the word I learned from Elene for holy bread.

My aunt couldn't fast the Lent the lump in her breast metastasized. She had to go on life support—a thick, milky substance pumping into her stomach from a hanging plastic bag. Before her brain died, Elene asked for *qurbana*. During the liturgy, I watched the priest break the round loaf along the cross shape the deacons had made as they were chanting prayers over the rising dough, and blowing on it—the mystery breath-of-life Elene believed turns bread into body. I brought a piece of *qurbana* back to her hospital room. But Elene couldn't swallow anymore. She was barely living—on *naemat allah*, the grace of God.

Macarona Béchamel

Serves 8 to 10

3 T. butter or ghee (clarified butter)
4 heaping T. all-purpose flour, sifted
3 c. cold milk
Salt and white pepper
1 egg, slightly beaten (optional)
3 T. butter or ghee
1 sm. yellow onion, finely diced
½ lb. ground beef
2 T. tomato paste (optional)
1 lb. (16 oz.) long tubular noodles sold in Greek and Lebanese food shops;
  ziti can be substituted

Béchamel Sauce

1. Melt butter (or ghee) in heavy-bottomed saucepan until foam subsides, watching carefully so it does not burn. Remove from heat.
2. Add sifted flour, stirring well with wooden spoon.
3. Return saucepan to burner. Over medium heat, stir mixture continuously three to four minutes (not allowing flour to brown). Remove from heat.

4. In medium saucepan, bring milk to boil. Then add to flour and butter mixture off heat, beating quickly with whisk.
5. Return saucepan to low/medium heat and bring to boil, stirring constantly to prevent lumps from forming.
6. After mixture reaches boiling point, cook five to seven minutes more until all flour is dissolved. Mixture should have moderate consistency. Add milk if too thick, small amount of flour if thin. Add salt and pepper to taste.
7. If using beaten egg, stir in now. Remove saucepan from heat.

Casserole

1. Preheat oven to 350°F.
2. In medium-sized skillet over medium heat, melt butter or ghee and carefully sauté onions only until yellow. Add ground beef, breaking up with wooden spoon, season with salt and pepper, and brown until no pink shows (20 to 25 minutes).
3. If using tomato paste, add now.
4. Boil noodles/ziti in salted water according to package directions and drain.
5. Grease nine by thirteen-inch metal pan (at least three inches deep).
6. Mix noodles/ziti with one cup béchamel sauce. Put half mixture in bottom of pan. Add layer of meat, followed by layer of other half of béchamel-noodle/ziti mixture. Top with remaining béchamel.
7. Bake until top is golden brown (30 to 45 minutes; check every 15 minutes). Remove and let settle for ten minutes, cut into squares and serve.

HOT MILK CAKE AND DISCOVERING MEMORIES

Lucy M. Long

Both my mother and grandmother were wonderful cooks. I remember sitting at their tables in Kannapolis, North Carolina, eating until I felt I would burst, and then crying because I couldn't eat more. They poured vast amounts of love and nurturing into their cooking, always aware of individual preferences of family members and making little concessions that spoke to that person.

I also remember times when my grandmother would leave church early on Sundays, missing the coffee social, to prepare the weekly dinner, and occasions when my mother, painting a sunset, stayed outside through the 6 p.m. dinner hour, apologizing profusely afterwards. Similarly, I remember times when the eaters did not show appreciation to the cook—and the hurt feelings afterwards. Cooking was both an avenue for artistic expression and a dutiful chore, a symbol of both selfless love and oppression.

Despite my heritage, I am not much of a cook. The oppressive side of cooking was what registered most. It was officially women's domain. And it couldn't be slapdash—it had to demonstrate thought and time and care. Cooking to me meant coming in early to prepare supper while my three brothers stayed outside playing, spending long amounts of time perfecting a dish and then watching it consumed in the blink of an eye—or left as a testimony to failure if it didn't suit tastes.

My attitude changed when I had my own children. I wanted to nurture them in the same way my mother had us. Besides, I discovered it was fun to create tasty dishes and gratifying to watch my family enjoy them. I began remembering how my mother would make pancakes in different animal shapes for each one of us or in the initials of our names. She also created signature dishes for each child—split pea soup, potato salad, and, I'm almost embarrassed to admit, green Jell-O and cottage cheese salad for me. Birthdays were the pinnacle of family celebration. The birthday child got to choose the menu, and my mother created a cake in a design of their choice—castles, trains, cats, paramecia, dinosaurs, and violins.

I celebrated in a similar way for my own children. That's when I realized that my mother's cake was special. She sent me her recipe for "Hot Milk Cake," noting that the name was a misnomer because if the milk was too hot it would kill the baking powder.

However, her signature cake did not become a lasting tradition in my family. One child didn't like it, another became an adamant vegan, and ironically, my daughter preferred store-bought ice-cream cakes. (She knew I hated shopping and processed foods, so she felt it was more a sign of my love to go to the store than stay home and bake.)

I put aside my mother's cake recipe and thought little more about it until I began research on family recipes. The annual birthday cake came immediately to mind, particularly the violin-shaped one she made for my 16th birthday and the map of Southeast Asia for my 19th. Several months ago, from my home in Bowling Green, Ohio, I asked my mother not only for the recipe but also for the story behind it. She was thrilled. It was an acknowledgment of the value and worth of her baking. It also led to some surprises for me. As she told me about the cake, I realized that her "voice" had been unheard, and that this item had much to tell me about my family heritage.

I had no idea that the recipe had come from my grandmother. In fact, it was one of the few that my mother had acquired from her. She, my grandmother, was born in 1917 in a small town in the Piedmont region of North Carolina. The family was "bluestocking Presbyterian" of Scottish ancestry. This meant a rather austere life, including restrictions against cooking, sewing, or shopping on Sunday. She married my grandfather, whose family name was Bradford, and who came from a long lineage going back to the *Mayflower*. The family farm was on land deeded to the Bradfords by King George IV prior the Revolutionary War. The family was well-off and respectable, but not overly rich. My grandfather worked as a supervisor of a cotton mill in the nearby town of Kannapolis, NC. That's where my mother grew up.

My mother remembers that as a child there was usually "help" for the cooking and housework. "Help" meant African-American women, many descended from slaves owned by my ancestors. Everything was made from scratch; including fried chicken that started with chasing the chicken. There was also less variety to the food than is available today: no broccoli or tropical fruits, no ethnic dishes, no fusion cuisine. Meals were family events, including lunch—when her father came home from the mill and my mother rode her bike home from school.

My mother wasn't allowed in the kitchen much—she might make a mess, and the hired help was there to help my grandmother. She didn't learn to cook until high school home economics classes. After several disasters, she mastered egg custard, a dish she continues to make to this day. She continued to cook because she likes to eat and make things. After having six children, it also became a necessity in order to feed the family. Now with 17 grandchildren, she still enjoys cooking for family occasions, sometimes making items like gingerbread with hot lemon sauce, also from her childhood, or dishes that she picked up from various sojourns in Asia and the Middle East. She is no longer defined by her cooking, but it is something that she uses to stir memories, strengthen relationships, and remind us of the connections we all share. Hot milk cake will now take on that role for me.

Hot Milk Cake

Serves 12

4 eggs
2 c. sugar

2 c. all-purpose flour, sifted
2 t. baking powder
Salt
1 T. butter, more for greasing
1 c. whole milk
1 t. vanilla or almond extract

1. Preheat oven to 350°F.
2. Butter and flour a nine by 12-inch cake pan or two eight-inch round or square pans.
3. With electric mixer on low, beat eggs until frothy. Gradually add sugar. Beat until thickened.
4. In separate bowl, re-sift flour with baking powder and pinch of salt.
5. In small saucepan, melt butter.
6. Add milk and heat to warm (Do not boil!!). Remove from heat and add flavoring extract.
7. Fold dry and wet ingredients gently into egg mixture in three alternating additions.
8. Bake about 30 minutes, until cake is brown around edges.
9. Remove from oven and allow to cool on wire rack.
10. Cut into desired shapes, and ice with favorite icing.

EDITH, GUSSIE AND LINZER TORTE

Gillian Polack

I have a very particular recipe book. Most of the time, the recipes document my life, travels, family, and the culinary exploits of my friends. Some are special. The one for linzer torte, for instance, came originally from Edith Phillips, my father's cousin-by-marriage. She was born Edith Deutsch, and fled Vienna just ahead of the Holocaust.

Edith came from a cosmopolitan, metropolitan, highly cultured Jewish community to a minute and very British one in Melbourne, (Victoria) Australia, in 1938. I've modified the recipe to suit a warmer climate and my own taste, but I shall always tell the story as she told it to me.

Edith trained as a doctor in Germany, but had to work as a private nurse when she came to Australia because of restrictions imposed on those trained overseas. She obtained work as an invalid nurse with Augusta Polack (Gussie), my great aunt, whose husband was ill.

Eventually, she married Gussie's son, Albert. The family was (and is) big and unstructured and more Anglo-British than European.

All the Polack-Phillips women were good cooks in the Australian style, but it wasn't the cookery Edith was used to. She explained to me that Gussie wanted to throw out a perfectly good joint after making soup. Edith rescued it before it became garbage, saying, "There's still meat on this."

Edith and Gussie argued about food quite a bit. My favorite anecdote tells of Edith looking despairingly at the standard meal of roast, vegetables, and pudding and saying, "If only I had my books, I could cook you real food."

"I don't need books in order to cook," retorted Gussie.

I come from that Australian family that Edith discovered. She was a very important influence in my life, helping my sisters and me develop a strong understanding of scientific method (I remember a drawer full of articles on cannabis, so I could decide for myself whether I should be interested), a good appreciation of Persian rugs and formal gardens, an understanding—if we had to flee our homeland—what would make our lives tolerable when we started over (she recommended a Persian rug, but any single object carried from the old home to the new country would help), and a very precise notion of afternoon tea.

Her cakes were Continental. All the food she served us was from pre-war Vienna, rather than Melbourne in the '60s and '70s. Edith's food was exotic to us.

Some years ago, when I was visiting Victoria from New South Wales, Edith asked me to drop in. This was the last time I saw her alive.

She told me that she was tidying her legacies. She showed me photos and family materials and told me stories that she had previously kept very close.

"There's something I'd like to give you," she said. "You understand the history and you can cook. I want these remembered."

Her sons have the originals, but she gave me copies of several recipes she had carefully preserved. They were from her mother.

When the photographs were away and we were sitting down over a cup of tea, she told me the tale of the linzer torte recipe. That story explained why it was so important that she have a female relative—even if it was one by marriage and from an alien culture—to carry the story and occasionally make the cake.

I always think of it as a "once upon a time" story, the sort of tale that goes well with a cup of good coffee and piece of linzer torte, shiny with butter and sweet with good jam.

Once upon a time, there was a Jewish family in Vienna. It was World War I and the wife was relieved that her soldier-husband was guarding the aqueducts rather than serving at the Front. Edith said that she imagined herself, barely able to walk, becoming tangled in her mother's skirts and driving her mother to distraction. She said this with such great satisfaction that I know it was true.

One day, news came. Edith's father was going to be sent to the Russian Front. Soon. Or it might have been a rumor. Either way, Edith's mother was scared.

You see, she wasn't just any housewife in Vienna with a husband in the army. She was Hungarian and Jewish. If he left, she would be entirely alone, in a place she really didn't know well, without any family or friends, and terrified that the next person she met might hate her, just for her religion. She was worried about herself, but, more than that, she was terrified for her two little children.

Someone had told her that the wife of the governor was also Hungarian. Edith's mother saw a ray of hope.

She went to the governor's residence and asked if she could speak to his wife. Next thing she knew, she and her babies were sharing coffee with the lady herself. She was very distressed, but the governor's wife was reassuring. She said she would do what she could to keep Edith's father in Vienna. She sent Edith's mother away with her very own recipe for linzer torte and many reassurances. She signed the recipe with a flourish.

It was a powerful recipe: the Deutsch family remained in Vienna until Edith fled the Nazis, twenty-odd years later.

Whenever I find myself overwhelmed by the hate in the world, I make this recipe and remember the compassion of the governor's wife. I remember Edith and how she taught me not to take things at face value and not to let the effect of others' hate burden my own life. I slow down and smile, in tribute to the three strong women this recipe represents: Edith, Gussie, and the governor's wife.

I don't work from the recipe directly. The Polack family notion of recipes (that Auntie Gussie also practiced) is that they should inspire cooking, but not prescribe it. I use an adaptation that started with Edith's own translation and that I have changed to meet my life needs. So the story of Edith's family meets with my family's foodways and a slightly different cake emerges every time.

Edith would have had me analyze this to understand it. Her gifts to the family were vast. She gave us a sense of humanity, of thinking, of analysis. She also gave us some very good cake recipes.

Linzer Torte

Serves 6

1 c. sugar
1 ½ c. butter
1 c. all-purpose flour
1 c. ground almonds
1 egg
1 t. of favorite spices (e.g. cinnamon, nutmeg)
Zest of ½ lemon, finely chopped
Raspberry jam (½ to 1 c., depending on desired sweetness)

1. Preheat oven to 375°F.
2. In medium bowl, mix together sugar, flour, and almonds.
3. Rub butter with flour lightly, until mixture has fine, even texture.
4. Set about one-quarter of dough aside for lattice strip decorations. Press remainder about one-quarter-inch deep into two greased and floured nine-inch square baking pans.
5. Spread jam evenly over pastry.
6. Cut lattice strips from remaining dough and lay them diagonally and horizontally across top.
7. Bake for 15 minutes, then lower temperature to 325°F, and bake for another 15 minutes.
8. Place linzer tortes on wire racks to cool, and then cut into squares.

AND FOR TONIGHT'S PERFORMANCE. . .

Ellen Kaye

To say that my husband's mother and I had an icy relationship is putting it mildly. Wild about his ex, she had no interest in getting to know me, or letting me know her. I can count our face-to-face encounters on one hand, and remember them as if they were yesterday. Our most successful get-together was the one time she came for dinner at our New York City brownstone, and limited her critique to our lack of living room curtains. The worst was a holiday gathering at a restaurant in suburban Westchester County, New York, that began with her unjustly accusing me of taking her spot at the table, and ended shortly after with her dramatic exit, inhibited solely by the parking lot post into which she smashed the rear end of her car.

So it seems somewhat apropos that the only gift this woman ever gave me was a very sharp cooking knife, which I tried hard not to interpret as *too* much of an insult, considering that one of the rare good things her children ever said about her was that she was an amazing cook. While other kids were eating Shake 'n Bake and Hamburger Helper, my husband and his sisters were feasting on Beef Wellington and linzer torte. Perhaps—I tried to think kindly at the time—the knife was an attempt to inspire me. Maybe it was her way of encouraging me to show my love to her son in the only way she, herself, knew how. But her difficult personality, and the toll it took on her offspring, left me wary.

After she died, one of the few things my husband claimed from his mother's belongings was her massive cookbook collection that he promptly shoved into a corner of our library. The cartons had been gathering dust for years before I actually took a look.

It was a dark winter afternoon, with hours to kill before my husband would be home. Newly unemployed, I was trying to regain a sense of accomplishment by systematically attacking our apartment's detritus, room by room. I spied the cookbooks stacked against a back wall and, as was my habit, became immediately distracted. From Mexican to Hungarian, just about any craving could be sated from the assortment. Curious about her personal favorites, I went straight to the three-ringed binders filled with recipes she had clipped, sent away for from daytime talk shows, and hand-copied in her meticulous European script. Much to my surprise, I began to spot a theme. There, tucked between the *Langue de Boeuf aux Lentilles* and the Crème Brûlée, were Paul Lynde's Stew, Shirley Temple's Quick Dinner, and Connie Stevens' Chicken *à la Pappa*.

Now, I can understand some starry-eyed small town housewife aspiring to cook like the stars, but my husband's mother had been a fairly well known actress in her heyday. An ingenue in Vienna, she had impressively parlayed her talent to a modest success on Broadway and in Hollywood. So why the draw to Robert Wagner's Corn Skillet or J. Edgar Hoover's Popovers, especially for a woman who had mastered *Meringues Glacées* and Lobster Mousse?

My husband didn't have a clue. He harbored vague memories of his mother dramatically presenting dishes in a CorningWare casserole or on a silver platter, claiming they were some famous person's favorite, though he admits that he never quite understood all the fuss.

I turned to his twin sister for enlightenment. "Celebrity dishes? My mother?" she asked incredulously. "No way. She would have never been into that kind of thing."

But the recipe collection proved otherwise. So I decided to try an experiment. I'd prompt my husband's sensory memory by making some of the dishes to see if I could unlock this mystery. First stop: Creole Red Kidney Beans with Rice à la Mrs. Louis Armstrong.

"Um, maybe she admired him because he was black?" he suggested, picking at the ham hock bobbing in the center of his bowl. I reminded him about those J. Edgar Popovers, and that Shirley Temple recipe. Neither his mother's support for civil rights nor her liberal politics seemed a likely match.

Ratatouille Newman, with its jarred tomato sauce (not Newman's Own) and pimiento-stuffed green olives, evoked another theory. "Oh, I know she respected Joanne Woodward as an actress."

"Then how do you explain Paul Lynde?" I shot back.

"Well, she really liked *Hollywood Squares*."

A dinner of Jill St. John's Chicken and Peppers, followed by a dessert of Mrs. Lyndon Johnson's Famous Lemon Cake, provided nothing, except unwanted weight from all the butter.

"I don't know," sighed my husband later that evening. "Maybe she trusted these people because they were fellow celebrities. Or maybe it was her way of staying connected to them. Can't we just have some grilled tuna tomorrow?"

I carefully tucked the recipe books back into their corner. But I couldn't get the last thing he said out of my mind. I felt he might be on to something. If his mother was spending long mornings clipping recipes, and lazy afternoons tuning in for guest chefs on the *Mike Douglas Show*, not to mention faithfully attending the nightly preparation of the family dinner, she wasn't exactly running off to auditions or rehearsals.

I sat there for a minute, picturing my mother-in-law in her suburban kitchen, carefully staging her culinary productions with the help of her ersatz co-stars, anticipating the applause of her husband and teenaged children, by then her only audience. And while I heard the sound of our messy bedroom closet calling my name, I chose to ignore it, instead turning to the hefty copper and gold volume of Vincent and Mary Price's *Treasury of Great Recipes*. Tomorrow? Maybe I'll give their Sherbet Castle a try.

Shirley Temple Black's Quick Dinner

Crisco oil
½ lb. lean ground beef
1 c. onions, chopped
1 pkg. frozen spinach (10 oz.)

4 eggs
Salt and pepper to taste

1. In large frying pan over medium heat, heat oil. Brown meat and onions, breaking up meat with side of wooden spoon. Drain spinach and add. Add eggs and stir until dish is thoroughly cooked through. Season with salt and pepper.

BAKMOY

Ditte Lokon

My grandmother was a keeper of keys. She always carried a small wicker basketful. The keys opened all sorts of doors to all sorts of goodies. There were very specific times when she opened doors and we got a glimpse or taste of what was inside; otherwise, those doors remained locked. In the last few years of her life, she moved around the house with a cane in each hand. As much as we wished she would leave her basket behind, she always found ways to bring it along, the handle pushed back to her elbow.

My sister and I kept an eye on one very important key that opened a very special cupboard, full of Indonesian and Dutch goodies. *Sumpia abon* (finger-sized, deep-fried egg roll snacks filled with dried meat), coconut cookies, pineapple-filled shortbread, meringues, Dutch licorice candy (the black and salty kind), and Dutch butterscotch candy (*hopjes*).

My grandparents lived in Bandung in west Java, about four hours through the mountains from where we lived in Jakarta. At the time in Bandung, there were several Dutch pastry shops selling delicacies made with butter and cream—different from the Indonesian coconut-milk based sweets, wrapped in banana leaves.

We always looked forward to visiting because Oma took such pleasure in feeding us. One of her dishes was her version of the Chinese-Indonesian soup, *bakmoy*. Preparations began right after breakfast and ended only with serving at dinner. We were both in elementary school when this tradition began. It continued each time we came back to visit, even many years later after my sister and I had left home for college in California.

The first stage of our *bakmoy* morning began with dicing some of the ingredients into small quarter–inch cubes. Pork fat and chicken skin needed to be cubed to render fat. The fried pork and chicken skin were then used as crispy toppings. Firm tofu cubes were fried until crispy on the outside, while still soft inside. Shrimp, well, all special dishes needed to have some shrimp, cubed or not.

Oma's kitchen was on a covered patio outside her dining room. She worked at a stand-alone kerosene stove with blackened pots on the shelves. In mid-morning, we had our first scheduled snack that depended on what Opa had found at the market that morning. Sometimes we had *kelepon*, steamed rice cake filled with palm sugar and shredded coconut. Sometimes we had *rujak*, young mangoes, and other tangy, in-season fruits dipped in chili and palm sugar paste.

After our morning snack, the *bakmoy* production had to be put on hold while Oma prepared lunch.

After lunch, it was time to make the stock; chicken pieces and bones were simmered with the rendered fat. Then we all took naps, including Oma and Opa. We always hoped that Oma would forget to take her basket of keys with her, but she never did, until she died! After our nap was *the* time my sister and I always awaited eagerly when Oma opened the goodies cupboard and we would be allowed to choose a couple of snacks. My sister and I spent a lot of time talking about which ones we would try the following day. We strategized that by choosing different items and cutting each in half, we could sample more.

After the second snack, it was time to go back to the kitchen and attend the broth. We helped shred the chicken, or sometimes played hopscotch. Whatever we did, we were always within smelling distance of the *bakmoy*.

The final assembly happened just before we sat down for dinner. Opa said grace and served us rice. He passed each plate to Oma who ladled on the *bakmoy*. In addition to crispy pork and chicken skin toppings, we had bowls of chopped green onions, firecracker chilies, salty and sweet soy sauce, and fried shallots for garnishes.

Oma passed away while I was in school at Berkeley, struggling to learn to cook to satisfy my homesick palate. Although we never got hold of her keys, she did teach us the key to food appreciation: spend lots of time preparing because the anticipation lasts much longer than the devouring.

Bakmoy (Triple Delight Comfort Soup)

Serves 6

My mom and I worked on reconstructing the recipe together. She helped chop and dice, all the time muttering under her breath, "This is so much work. No wonder I never made it." We eyeballed quantities and measured amounts after-the-fact. Once we agreed on the process, I took notes. My dad and mom judged the result based on a taste memory of more than 20 years. They pronounced it a success!

2 whole chicken legs (about 1 ½ lb.)
1 ½ lb. pork bones
2 ½ qt. water
8 garlic cloves, peeled and sliced
½ lb. firm tofu, diced into ¼-inch cubes
½ lb. medium shrimp
3 T. fish sauce*
2 T. oyster sauce*
3 T. *kecap manis** (sweet soy sauce for which you can substitute a mixture
    of regular soy sauce and a little honey)
Salt and white pepper to taste
* *found in Asian markets*

For Garnish

Cilantro and green onions, chopped fine
Fried shallots
1 Thai red bird's eye chili pepper*, diced and crushed, and mixed into soy
    sauce as a condiment
* *found in Asian markets*

1. Remove skin from chicken legs. Fry over low heat (the skin will render its own fat), turning a few times until crispy. Reserve for topping and leave chicken fat in pan.
2. Fry pork bones until brown and place in four-quart soup pot.
3. Fry chicken legs until brown and add to soup pot.
4. Add water to soup pot, bring to boil, then reduce to whatever heat will just maintain a simmer.
5. When chicken legs are cooked through (about 15 minutes), remove from pot with tongs, cut meat off bones, and return bones to soup pot. Simmer about two hours.
6. When chicken has cooled, cut into half-inch cubes.
7. If there is any meat left on pork bones, remove and add to soup.
8. Discard all bones, both chicken and pork.
9. Add salt and white pepper to soup to taste. You may add a splash of fish sauce but not so much that the soup tastes of it. About 15 minutes before eating, start final preparatory steps:
10. Make rice.

11. Using chicken fat from step 1, fry diced tofu until crispy. Remove from pan.
12. Add more chicken fat to pan and fry sliced garlic. Dry cubed chicken and shrimp with paper towels, add them to pan, and fry until brown.
13. Add fried tofu and sauces (oyster, fish, and *kecap manis*). Sauté briefly for one to two minutes, turn off heat.

Note: *To serve, place rice in soup bowls. Ladle broth on top, followed by some chicken/shrimp/tofu, then sprinkle on garnishes (cilantro, green onions, and chicken skin bits), and serve.*

POST MORTEM PEACH SURPRISE

Annie Lanzillotto

Grandma Rose died at a hundred-and-a-half with two legs on, which is a garlic miracle. The surgeon and all the men in my family agreed she was too old at 99 for vascular surgery. Her blue, ice-cold leg must be amputated below the knee to relieve her of the constant pain about which she cried to San'Antonio.

I looked at the men in the waiting room of the emergency room at the Bronxville, New York, hospital: the surgeon, my brother, my cousin. We were all standing. I said, "Give me eight days. If the leg doesn't heal, then you can cut it off."

"It's only a piece of meat," my brother, the Marine, reassured me.

I telephoned my mother's companion, Al. "Go get me some of that strong garlic with the purple on its skin." Whenever I had no idea what to do, I did what my girlfriend, Audrey, told me she learned from a theater director, "When you don't know what to do, stand up and say, "This is what I want___", and something always comes out of your mouth right. So, I started giving orders. "Get the good oil. Get the good garlic." I had no idea what I would do with the garlic; I just knew that when it came to healing, my family believed in garlic. But, did I?

I had stuck a clove in my ear for an earache, rubbed some around my neck for a swollen throat, even applied some to my feet to breathe; garlic travels from your feet to your tongue, you can taste it. I was American with an Italian background that suddenly came to the foreground. When there was nothing left to be done, I took the garlic out. My Uncle Frank had always told me, "Garlic is the essence of life." Grandma Rose never paid for garlic; routinely pocketing bulbs at the supermarket. In homage to her, I'd written a play "Pocketing Garlic," in which one character says, "Some things in life you shouldn't pay for. Garlic is essential. Garlic is the essence of life. It will push an ocean through your aorta if you know how to eat it."

I wasn't going to let my grandmother who lived a whole century get mutilated just 'cause she ate too many jelly donuts. You see, Grandma Rose was in this predicament because when no one was looking, she stuffed herself with jelly donuts and downed espressos at the holiday meal. This on top of gorging figs from the neighbor's tree. A twisted intestine, emergency surgery, and three weeks in the post-op intensive care unit led to a blood clot and the death of her right leg.

For eight nights I kept vigil by her side. Audrey accompanied me each night. We crushed the garlic, smothered the leg with a fine coat of Vaseline, then virgin cold pressed olive oil and a garlic poultice, wrapping the leg in a white cotton pillowcase. In the morning I would wash the leg and let it breathe. After two nights of this ritual, the hospital put Grandma in a private room and the nurses stopped coming in because of the garlic stench the lesbians were causing. That's one way to get a private room! Audrey led Grandma in visualizations, "See the blood flowing freely," and Grandma would point to the spot on her leg where it hurt, saying "blooda clock." We could see the blood fill the veins like arroyos moving from concavity to convexity and back again. We held our hands' heat over the leg. When the family members visited, they too added the heat of their hands. Over the eight nights, everyone in the family, even the unbelievers, had added the heat of their hands and joined in the Ave Marias.

At the end of eight days and nights, Grandma marched out of the hospital. Nurses stunned. Doctors silent. She lived and died intact, over a year later. When she did finally emigrate to heaven, I had this American brainstorm to plant a tree in her name. I tried to collect money from the family. But Grandma Rose had called me *Education Girl, Accomplishment Nothing*, and in this endeavor she proved right. I couldn't gather the money or execute the plan. She died in March. That May a peach tree sprouted just outside my mother's living room window, perfectly centered among Mom's three contiguous windows, right where Grandma Rose tossed her peach pits out the window after dinner. It was as if she was saying, "Useless AmeriCAHN! I will do it myself!" and further taunting me that you don't need money or collaboration to plant a tree—just connection to yourself and the earth, that connection that she had as a young peasant that made the dry earth give birth. I felt her soul transmogrify into a peach tree.

The first year Grandma gave us two peaches. By the fifth year, she was over two stories high and gave 33 peaches. We ate their sweetness raw. This year the tree is eight years old, and delivered a thousand peaches, which we blanched and froze and ate through the winter. When I prune the tree, my mother and I save the branches because to us, they are Grandma's legs. The branches hold our laundry in the shower, hang out on the fire escape; I carry one around as a walking stick. We save the pits also, toss them on the grass sides of highways and fields for more trees to grow, others we wear as talismans of Grandma's spiritual power. I gave peaches out at the Black Madonna Festival in the East Village, and poet Gabriella Belfiglio planted a pit in Brooklyn that has sprouted into a baby tree.

The peaches grow in clumps, "like grapes" my mother says. The mailman and neighbors freely eat off the tree. For recipes, my mom called her cousin, my Aunt Lucy, in Yonkers, New York, who is smart in all ways, especially in the kitchen. Aunt Lucy gave us this recipe. Lucy collects recipes from all over, and doesn't recall what heritage this is from, but the directions are precise, and it is wonderful. And Grandma's peaches deserve multi-cultural recipes; she was the first in the family to try tofu, calling it "mozzarella Cinese," and she always wanted something new to eat. So here it is Grandma, yet another way to eat your peaches.

Peach *Kuchen*

Serves 6

1 ½ c. sifted flour
¼ t. baking powder
½ t. salt
1 c. sugar
6 T. butter
6 ripe peaches, halved and pitted
⅛ t. nutmeg
1 t. cinnamon
2 egg yolks
1 c. heavy cream

1. Preheat oven to 400°F.
2. Sift flour, baking powder, salt, and two tablespoons sugar together. Work in butter with fork until mixture looks like cornmeal. Pile into an eight-inch ungreased, square pan and, with fingers, pat an even layer over bottom and halfway up sides. Place peach halves, cut side down, over pastry. Sprinkle on mixture of sugar and cinnamon and bake 15 minutes.
3. Remove from oven. In small bowl, mix yolks and cream together and pour over *kuchen*. Bake 30 minutes or until golden. Remove from oven, cut into six squares and serve warm.

BLACK RASPBERRY PIE AND CRUSTY WOMEN

Tamara Sharp

You wouldn't think that the ability to make Black Raspberry Pie would determine your role in life, but thanks to my paternal grandmother, that's exactly what happened. Rhea Enright Genson (1904–1987) made Black Raspberry Pie from memory and love. Grandmother Extraordinaire, Superwoman before the term was coined, she cooked and baked with élan, using food and meals to incorporate the seemingly incompatible ingredients of our large, blended family into a real family—a genuine, no-special-adjective-required family.

Tamara Sharp's paternal grandmother Rhea Enright Genson cuts the birthday cake she made for Tamara and her cousin Lissa in 1971. © Tamara Sharp. Used by permission.

Every weekend, after work on Saturdays and church on Sundays, at her home in Haskins, Ohio (population less than 500), she made big dinners for my three brothers, my two stepbrothers, my half-brother, my dad, my stepmother, my grandfather, my mentally retarded great-great aunt, me and . . . oh yeah, herself. Seven children and five adults were regularly fed their favorite foods, and, during leisurely meals, also fed important life lessons. Each was painstakingly blended into the family, shaken and stirred, patted and shaped as needed, until we were absorbed into Grandma's ideal of perfection: a Black Raspberry Pie-loving Family, emphasis firmly on *Family*.

Grandma's Black Raspberry Pie recipe was, of course, special, because in her eyes we were special, and therefore, not just any old black raspberry pie would do. It had to be the perfect, flaky-crusted, juicy-but-not-soggy, freshly-hand-picked-berries kind, made exactly according to her recipe. Well, it's sort of a recipe: one of those "a pinch of this," "a dab of that" recipes with measurements guesstimated at the insistence of others, a dish impossible to recreate on your own, unless you happen to be the person chosen by Grandma to carry on the tradition.

Why she chose me for that role, I'll never know. Half tomboy, half book-worm, I had little interest in what I disdainfully called "Suzy Homemaker stuff." But I could never resist a challenge; in hindsight, I think that may be why she chose me. Not just anyone can produce a primo Black Raspberry Pie, after all, let alone an honest-to-God Family. It takes determination, ingenuity, persistence, and a refusal to quit when life—or piecrust—gets tough.

Grandma's pie recipe was deceptively simple: only three ingredients, but when you looked closely, you saw there were actually five. Well, okay, six, if you count the handmade crust which, despite the fact that it's crucial, was not even listed. In fact, it's mostly the things that aren't in the recipe that really matter. You have to know, for instance, that it's a two-crust pie, that the crust must be flaky, and that the top crust should be artfully slit for ventilation, and also coated with milk and sprinkled sugar so it will glisten. You have to know that approximately three cups of freshly picked berries are needed. They must be checked individually and ruthlessly for flaws, carefully rinsed (never soaked!) in cold water, and thoroughly drained. You must know that the amount of sugar needs to be adjusted according to the tartness or sweetness of the berries. You should know how much salt is in a dash (a calculation that depends on the size of the shaker top and number and size of holes). Too much injures the taste, while not enough disappoints the palate, and you have to know the quantity, proper thickness, and correct placement of the butter dots (that aren't really dots at all), on top of the berry mixture, but underneath the top crust and away from where the slits will be. Finally, you have to know that the pie goes on the middle oven rack so that it browns properly on top, but not at all on the bottom, and that a cookie sheet should be placed beneath to catch any berry spill. Although, of course, if you've done everything correctly, there won't be any.

The real secret is in the crust.

Sometimes I think that's what we are, my Grandma and me: the family crusts. She's the bottom, the foundation on which everything depends, the invisible support system that props us all up. I'm the top, whose purpose is to hold everything together. I lack Grandma's grace and serenity; I am, rather, socially awkward and tense—crusty, in fact. I'm the crusty woman who sends birthday, graduation, and anniversary cards, as well as e-mails and letters to the rest of the family, the one who coordinates family gatherings and gift exchanges, and in so doing, continually tries to keep everyone informed about and caring about each other, in spite of the fact that we now live in several widely dispersed parts of the country, and our ranks have swelled at least three-fold by marriages, remarriages, and births. Naturally, I also bake excellent Black Raspberry Pies.

Except for the years I don't. Since Black Raspberry Pie is my dad's favorite, I make it every year for Father's Day, or as soon thereafter as the berries ripen. A few years ago, the local crop failed, and the absence of our traditional pie left a hole in our year, much as Grandma's death many years earlier left a hole in our lives. There was no pie that year, either. But the year my mom died, I managed to make the pie for Father's Day, just 11 weeks after her funeral. In the fugue state that accompanies overwhelming grief, I mixed baking soda instead of salt into the berries. The pie looked perfectly fine. The top crust was flaky and lightly browned, and the berry juice oozed sweetly through the perfectly-placed slits. But on the inside, the pie was absolutely awful, completely unrecognizable—just like me, for most of the next four years.

Long after Grandma had gone to her reward, she is still holding the family together with memories and Black Raspberry Pie, and I'm trying, rather unevenly, to fill her role. I have not yet chosen a pie-baking successor, or even taught my daughters. One lacks the patience, the other interest—so far, anyway. On the other hand, I think they understand what it is to *be* the family crust, and some day, perhaps, one or maybe both together will assume Grandma's and my role. Black raspberries, grandmothers, and daughters.

Black Raspberry Pie

Serves 8

You'll need pastry for a two-crust pie, with slits in the top crust to allow the steam to escape and the mouthwatering aroma to flavor the air. Any basic pie crust will do; Grandma used lard, but I'm a Betty Crocker fan myself.

Mix

3 c. black raspberries, washed and carefully picked over
1 c. sugar (more or less, depending on sweetness of berries)
2 T. cornstarch, or 4 T. flour
Dash salt
Unsalted butter

1. Preheat oven to 400°F.
2. Line pie tin with bottom crust.
3. Place berries in medium bowl. Add sugar, cornstarch, and salt, and combine carefully.
4. Pour berry mixture into bottom crust and dot with butter.
5. Add top crust, cut three to four slits, and pinch or crimp edges together.
6. Bake for 40 to 50 minutes until lightly browned.
7. Remove from oven and cool on rack for at least an hour.
8. Cut into slices and serve.

BREAD FOR HOBOES

D'Arcy Smylie Randall

Non ignara mali, miseris succurrere disco. (Vergil, *Aeneid,* I, 630) "Having known misfortune, I hasten to help others."

Growing up in the 1930s in Jackson, Mississippi, my mother would find a hobo at the breakfast table, drinking coffee and eating my grandmother's homemade bread. Rising before dawn to bake loaves for her family, Lucile Pearson O'Brien (known as "Bitsy" throughout her 96 years}, gave the hobo the first cut. The newly-baked loaves were fresh out of their pans, cooling on racks, just as the sun defined the path from the chicken coop, across the backyard, to the kitchen steps.

Soon Bitsy discovered that her house carried a "hobo hieroglyphic," a symbol used by the homeless during the Depression to communicate things like "food here." Yet, she made no attempt to remove it; she wanted the hoboes to find her.

Lucile ("Bitsy") Pearson O'Brien and her husband Peter Anthony O'Brien in Nicaragua around 1916 where Bitsy began her breadmaking. © D'Arcy Randall. Used by permission.

Bitsy was an outrageous misnomer for my mother's mother. She was in her eighties and living with us when I was a child, but her grandstanding frame scarcely contained her energy. She told stories of her life in such vivid detail that the events seemed to have just happened. These tales ripped us out of time, soaked us in 1916, or spun us down to the 1890s. I'd struggle to cast myself back to the 1970s.

When making bread, Bitsy would swoop down over the dough with her large hands, commanding it, yet respecting its life. The smell of the warm yeast baking in the oven filled the house so it was impossible to think of anything else. When she removed the loaves from the oven—torture. *Wait, it has to cool,* she'd insist. Finally, she cut the heel, sliced off a steaming, drooping piece, and held it out. The bread filled my stomach and soul.

Bitsy began making bread in 1916 in the remote northern mountains of Nicaragua at the Constancia gold mine. She was 34, and newly wed to an Australian engineer who managed the mine. My grandmother's marriage to Pete O'Brien, a foreign stranger, shocked her family. As a young woman, she had rebuffed so many suitors that by the time she was 30, there was no man left in Jackson, Mississippi, to turn down. Quite simply, she did not love them.

Her older sisters, married and living in Texas, assumed that Bitsy would stay home and care for their widowed mother, Miss Jennie. A visit to New Orleans, however, changed that when Bitsy met Pete, who had sailed up from Nicaragua to consult with the mine owner. Back in the tropics, he corresponded with my grandmother.

The following year, he returned to the United States, took Bitsy to a jewelry store, and asked the manager to show them diamond rings. She was stunned; Pete, taken aback by her reaction. After all, he thought he had proposed by letter and she had accepted. The letters are long-lost, but Pete's manner of expression was subtle, and Bitsy did not recognize that the laconic Australian was proposing. In contrast, Bitsy's letters were always high-spirited. I suspect the hopeful Pete read her naturally enthusiastic tone as a "yes." They did have to leave the store, temporarily, to sort things out.

After a honeymoon in New Orleans, she and Pete sailed to Nicaragua, and traveled up the coast by banana boat to the mouth of the Prinzapolka River. They spent weeks canoeing through the jungle, then rode muleback over a mountain to the mine.

In the house that Pete built on the jungle's edge, Bitsy taught herself to make bread. Ninety-year-old photographs show a radiantly happy couple. When local mine managers congregated, Bitsy shared her bread and the recipe with their wives. A Creole woman named Suzanne arrived to help Bitsy keep house, and according to Bitsy, developed an even better version of the bread. Bitsy and Pete lived at the mine for four years until 1919, when the price of gold fell and the Constancia was closed. Sadly, Pete and Bitsy—then pregnant with my mother—rode mules back over the mountain and canoed down the Prinzapolka for the steamer to New Orleans. For the rest of their lives, they'd evaluate a person's merit with the meaningful question, "Would you go upriver with her or him?"

After my mother was born, the three moved in with Miss Jennie in Jackson, and Pete found engineering work. While running the house and a small real-estate business, Bitsy made bread. The year the Depression hit, Miss Jennie developed cancer, and Bitsy cared for her.

With Miss Jennie's death, Bitsy turned inward. She no longer loved parties and people; she avoided church; stopped visiting and receiving friends. But she never stopped making bread. Although she refused to answer the front doorbell, she would open the kitchen door at dawn for a hobo emerging from the shadows. I suppose the breaking of bread with a hungry stranger may have been a way to live out her religious beliefs. Like Vergil's Dido, the visible anguish of these men resonated with her own suffering.

Bitsy's depression finally lifted in 1941 when my mom married. Pete died in 1947, and Bitsy lived for another 32 years, making bread until she could no longer see, or stand alone.

Bitsy's Bread

Makes 2 loaves

This recipe is the result of collaboration between my two grandmothers, Bitsy and Dora. Bitsy was notoriously impressionistic in cooking instructions, so on one occasion, Dora watched and took notes which produced this recipe.

2 c. milk
1 pkg. yeast (¼ oz.)
4 T. shortening
1 t. salt
¼ c. sugar
About 2 c. flour with extra for adding later and sprinkling on pastry board

1. Into large bowl, pour one cup milk. Add salt and sugar, and stir to mix. Set on warm stove top until lukewarm.
2. Dissolve yeast in one cup tepid milk and soak until yeast softens and looks foamy.
3. Add yeast/milk to salt, sugar, and milk mixture.
4. Add enough flour (about two cups) to give mixture consistency of cake batter.
5. Beat well with wooden spoon, cover with cloth, and let rise until doubled in bulk, about one- and-one-half hours.

6. Add enough additional flour to make dough workable (not too sticky) and knead well on floured board for 12 to 15 minutes.
7. Put in large bowl and grease top of dough with butter. Allow dough to rise again until doubled in bulk, about one hour.
8. Preheat oven to 350°F. Grease two metal loaf pans.
9. Knead dough one more time for about 10 minutes, divide in two and place each half into a loaf pan.
10. Bake for 30 minutes in gas oven (slightly longer for electric).
11. Remove and let rest for 10 minutes, then tip loaves out. Allow to cool on metal racks and slice.

As we connect with life lessons through storied dishes, we refine our identities—who we are. Plumbing the deep reservoirs of our way of being, our woman's consciousness, we tap into wisdom we can use throughout our lives.

5

Bonding Together

I always enjoy it when someone gives me a recipe that he or she is passionate about; it is a real connection with that person. There is something communal about having shared recipes, about passing tastes and flavors from friend to friend and from generation to generation.[1]
—Marion Cunningham, *Lost Recipes: Meals to Share with Friends and Family*

Food ties women together in special and long-lasting relationships. Friends who meet regularly over many years for a theme meal, multiple generations who whip up baked beans for family potlucks, and two women who use food as a bridge to reconcile their opposing food styles and further an intimate relationship. Favorite dishes become the essential glue. The pledge among women in a family never to divulge a secret recipe can become a bond in itself, encircling them in an exclusive relationship. Food strengthens our relationships with other women and reminds us of shared connections.

THE GARLIC GIRLS

Annie Hauck-Lawson

It was 1980 in New York City. *Garlic Is As Good As Ten Mothers* (a documentary about growing, cooking, and celebrating this beloved Allium) was playing at Film Forum in Manhattan. Watching it made me ravenous to eat a good, garlicky meal. It also made me hungry to cook one, so I instructed four garlic-passionate women friends with the signature monikers

Dog, Joy, n.garcia, and Rise (pronunced Rees-eh) to see the film and then come immediately to my house for dinner. (By the way, Dog is the nickname that my friend Ellen and I call each other, and n.garcia is the way another friend signed all her charts at work.) The *New York Times* food section had recently published a recipe for "Joe's Baked Garlic Soup." I prepared it, along with some other aromatic dishes. The tradition of "The Garlic Dinner" was born.

Early in each new year thereafter, we'd start murmuring that it was time for the Garlic Dinner. We'd pick a night; an apartment; and a course (soup, salad, entrée, dessert) for each to prepare . . . plus beer.

The annual dinners followed a format:

1. Wear our "Passionate for Garlic" T-shirts (hand-painted by me with two heads of garlic flanking the slogan).
2. Inhale the meal, figuratively and literally.
3. Drink very much beer.
4. Write a collective letter to filmmaker Les Blank, apprising him that the Garlic Dinner was upcoming, listing this year's menu, informing him that he was our garlic hero, and promising that if he was ever in New York, we would hold a Garlic Dinner in his honor, signed, "the Garlic Girls."
5. Deal with the dessert issue. Usually, by the end of the meal, we were ready to crash/dive into something yummily sweet like deep-dish fruit pies with crumb toppings and ice cream. We discussed "Garlic Ice Cream" from a theoretical perspective, but never went there.
6. Discuss the (aromatic) effects of garlic consumption in our daily lives (work, relationships, conversations), especially since each year we tried to top the previous with greater amounts. By year three, we were up to three heads each! The day after one Garlic Dinner, the aroma emanating from Joy prompted the evacuation of co-workers from her close-quartered office.
7. Pee in our pants. After the first Garlic Dinner, Dog brought her childhood friend, Sophie, into the fold; a great addition, as she happens to be one of the funniest people on Earth. The combination of garlic girls, garlic food, and beer with Sophie's over-the-top style, just about guaranteed item number seven.

One Friday, I was running my usual busy. Needing to travel to Manhattan from home in Brooklyn and also needing to prepare for the evening meal, I thought to "kill two birds with one stone" by using the subway as an opportunity to peel garlic. As riders got on and smelled what I was doing, they moved to more distant parts of the car.

One year, 1985, we got a reply from Les Blank. He WOULD be in town, speaking at a Friday night showing of his film. We slated a Garlic Dinner for the evening before and invited S.O.s (Significant Others)—that meant boys—our spouses or spouses-to-be. Electric with anticipation, we enhanced our normal preparation. Rise and John's centrally located Upper West Side apartment was aromatic with garlic-studded leg of lamb with rosemary, olive oil, and more garlic rub. The doorbell rang and we ran to the hallway, hearts pounding as elevator cables whirred. The doors opened and a huge giant-man stepped out. Our voices, collective yet tiny, uttered, "Hi, Les. We're the Garlic Girls," and an even tinier voice responded, "Hello."

Something about this particular meal was too much. Too much rich food, too much beer, too much uncontained excitement. We went to the theater the next night as pre-planned with toaster ovens, heads of garlic, olive oil, cognac, and paper fans, baking the garlic backstage and walking up and down the aisles, fanning the trays during key parts of the film, providing "Aroma-rama."

After that year, the Garlic Dinner went on hiatus. Things happened—we moved, we moved on, we lost touch with n.garcia. Joy's S.O. got sick and died. Some of us married, some had babies.

Then in 2004, Joy herself, still living in New York City, got sick, and Dog (Vermont), Rise (Connecticut), and I (Brooklyn), friends over the miles, encircled Joy in a tight friendship ring. For the next two years, we were connected like glue . . . on the telephone, in visits, over meals laced with garlic, in a *Big Chill* weekend, in containers of sauce and soup tucked into Joy's freezer, in thoughts and prayers, in overnights at Joy's apartment—always cleaned, organized, and re-stocked by Dog and Rise during their visits, or next to her bed at the hospital . . . our e-mails full of progress reports, were titled "Hey, G.G.s" as often as possible, when they weren't titled, "Bad news" and "More bad news."

In the summer of 2005, we traveled to Martha's Vineyard. At Joy's and her four-year-old-daughter Ava's summer cottage, we cooked a symbolic garlic dinner. The garlic was tame, but our hope, enthusiasm, and happiness in being together held no bounds, captured in photos of us holding lobsters triumphantly high above Joy's bald head, mile-wide smiles all around.

Yes, Joy died, and family, friends, and kids gathered at her memorial. Our kids, Alana and Phillip, Elise and Paul, and we Garlic Girls, with Rise's husband John and my husband Danny, sat in a close cluster. Here are some of my words to the group plus a recipe.

". . . Joy's and my friendship was ignited by our love for food–cooking, eating, seeking, exploring, reading, discussing recipes, and dishes. A fully chocolate meal preceded every annual excursion to the Bensonhurst Christmas lights with Diana and Daniel (Joy's niece and nephew), Alana, Phillip and, eventually–finally! Ava.

"Garlic cemented our friendship. Around 1980, the tradition of the 'Garlic Dinner' was born. The first meal included recipes from the *New York Times*. 'Joe's Baked Garlic Soup' was tame in comparison with dishes that followed."

After the Les Blank fest, the Garlic Dinner (in its original incarnation) actually never took place again. However, garlic continued to bind our passion for cooking, eating, and discussing food. And Garlic Dinners had been something we created and shared. I dedicate a "spin–off" of the soup served at the first Garlic Dinner to Joy, with love.

Joy's Baked Garlic Soup

2 to 3 garlic heads, separated into cloves and peeled
3 qt. strong, seasoned (preferably meat) broth
1 loaf French bread
Gruyère and grated pecorino romano cheese

1. Preheat oven to 450°F.
2. In four-quart stockpot over low heat, simmer garlic in broth for 20 minutes or until very soft and buttery.
3. Line bottoms of six ovenproof crocks with chunks of torn bread, distribute garlic cloves around and cover completely with hot broth. Top with shredded gruyère and pecorino romano to taste.
4. Bake until cheese melts and browns (less than 10 minutes). Remove crocks carefully—they will be very hot—and set one in front of each diner; dig in, and enJoy!

HOW I GOT MY *CHOLE* RECIPE—A WEDDING TALE

Rachelle H. Saltzman

Years ago, a good friend and folklorist told me that planning a wedding was like putting together a folklife festival. As a veteran of many festivals—since my job in Des Moines, Iowa, involves documenting Iowa's folk and traditional artists and their cultural traditions—I can attest that those years of work experience were critical for the multi-tasking necessary to produce a wedding for two mature adults with children, parents, other relatives, friends from around the United States, and one childhood buddy who flew in from New Zealand.

The multicultural potluck buffet table at Rachelle Saltzman's wedding reception. © Merri McKenzie. Used by permission.

But a wedding is considerably more emotionally laden than a festival, no matter how many performers, tents, and contingency plans the latter involves. As adults in our 50s, Nick and I were lucky to have supportive parents and children, as well as wonderful friends from our past lives in other places, our temple, Nick's music buddies, and the circle of folks who help me do my work. All were eager to be a part of our celebration. Yet some kind of reasonable budget was not an unimportant consideration.

My solution was a potluck and music jam. When I first suggested this, Nick, a professional musician and committed foodie, was a bit skeptical, not wanting to offend his musician friends by asking them to play for free—or have folks from afar deal with bringing a dish, as well as themselves and a present. What with combining households, the last thing we needed was more stuff, so I suggested that food and music contributions become the gifts. Nick started thinking it could work.

Our wedding started to take shape as a more organized version of my multicultural Chanukah potlucks. I fry lots of potato *latkes* (pancakes), and friends bring a dish from their culture or region, children, musical instruments, and a good appetite. Once my daughter—whom I brought home as a baby from Cambodia—arrived on the scene, holiday parties expanded into annual "gotcha day" events. (Many adoptive families have "gotcha day" celebrations to honor the day they "got" each other.) Friends would bring dishes that ranged from Asian Indian curries, Jell-O cake, and Chinese noodle dishes to mac and cheese, *Tai Dam* egg rolls, a memorable Barbie cake (a dome-shaped cake decorated like a skirt for the doll inserted in the center), Bosnian pita (a hot, strudel-like, meat, vegetable, or fruit-filled pastry), brownies, and Argentinean *empanadas* (meat pies).

Luckily, I have several type-A women friends, many of whom are great cooks and event organizers. About two months before the wedding, I invited them to brainstorm the final menu and taste test at a pre-wedding "food committee" meeting. Our only request was no *traif* (nonkosher, i.e., no shellfish, no pork, and no dishes that combined dairy and meat products). Besides pita and *empanadas*, Lao fresh rolls, and flourless chocolate cakes, one dish in particular stood out. My friend, Sherry Gupta, brought *chole* (an Indian chickpea stew). Sherry had married into an Asian Indian family, and the recipe came from Madhuri, her mother-in-law.

Sherry and I had met years before at a discussion on cultural diversity and discovered that we'd both worked on diversity days at our kids' schools. With that in common, we started talking, and our conversations about kids, husbands, spiritual issues, and food have never stopped. Sherry and her family started coming to our potlucks, and she and I started working together on World of Difference, her not-for-profit that promotes cultural diversity programs. She's become a dear friend, ever ready with warm hugs and an understanding smile.

Sherry's *chole* was a big hit, and immediately went on the wedding menu for the June date in 2007, in addition to Greek lamb meatballs with lemon sauce, *lukschen kugel* (a sweet egg noodle, cottage cheese, egg, and raisin pudding), egg rolls, tabbouleh, falafel, salads, *pilau* (a chicken and rice dish), cucumber sandwiches, fruit bowl, pickled asparagus, and poached salmon plus an array of cakes, pastries, and a chocolate fountain "for the kids" as well as the other dishes "approved" by the food committee. Of course, one of the perils of a wedding is that the bride and groom don't have much time to sit down and actually eat. The friend who was supposed to load up plates for us couldn't penetrate the crowds around the buffet tables.

We finally made our way to the spread only to find many of the platters empty! Luckily for us, there was still a huge amount of food, including some of that wonderful *chole*, which truly was something special—a lovely warming and comforting combination of chickpeas, onions, tomatoes, and savory spices, now a mainstay of our dinner table. While Mexican and Lao friends played music and danced for everyone, we ate the food that so many had lovingly and generously prepared. It was an extraordinary start to married life, surrounded by family and friends, our senses replete.

Madhuri's *Chole*

Serves 6 to 8 with four to six cups of cooked basmati rice (plus *raita* and mango chutney)

Chickpeas

Four 15 oz. cans chickpeas (this is a substitute for the original dried chickpeas)
6 c. water
3 orange pekoe tea bags
4 cloves
1 bay leaf
3 "big cardamom," aka *badi elaichi* (black cardamom)
1 t. roasted cumin powder

1. Rinse chickpeas and place in large pot with tea bags, cloves, bay leaf, cardamom, and water.
2. Simmer over medium heat about 30 minutes to soften chickpeas and blend flavors.
3. Discard tea bags and bay leaf.
4. Drain chickpeas AND reserve cooking liquid to use with gravy.

Gravy/*Masala*

¼ c. vegetable oil
1 t. roasted cumin powder
1 ½ lg. onions, sliced thinly
3 heaping T. tandoori paste (garlic/ginger paste from Indian food market)
1 lg. tomato, cut into chunks
3 T. *channa masala* spice mixture (from Indian food market)
2 heaping t. salt

1. In large (10 to 12-inch) cast-iron frying pan over medium-low heat, place one-quarter cup oil along with cumin powder and onions. Fry until golden brown, about 10 to 15 minutes.
2. Add ginger/garlic paste, stir, and cook for about five minutes.
3. Add tomatoes, *channa masala,* and salt, and cook for about 10 minutes.
4. Add chickpeas and one cup leftover liquid from chickpeas and simmer for 15 to 30 minutes. (This is a pretty forgiving dish, so cooking longer is never an issue.)

5. Fix and decide whether you want more liquid. If so, add some and cook for another 15 to 20 minutes—long enough for flavors to blend.

6. Serve with basmati rice, *raita,* and mango chutney on the side.

Sherry's comment: "It isn't a science. It's love. I hope your marriage is too. Hugs to the bride!"

MY LITTLE BLACK BOX

Janie Goldenberg

My recipe card box reads like a Rolodex. Thumbing through, I'm distracted by all the names: Leila's Hot Fruit Compote, Mindy's Brisket,

Janie Goldenberg's little black recipe box abounds with the names of many women. © Janie Goldenberg. Used by permission.

Nanny's Chopped Liver, Marjorie's Salad Dressing, Lila's Version of Joan's Cole Slaw, Arlene's Pasta Salad. Most of these women are no longer in my life. Some are dead. But all live with me in my kitchen in the Berkshire Mountains of Western Massachusetts.

My little black box holds secrets to simple comfort foods passed on from relatives and friends, through generations and history. Some probably shouldn't be called recipes at all. They are more like storytelling—oral history passed from mother to daughter. Their roots are perhaps even deeper. They thrive in their inexactitude—no measurements, just lists of ingredients that come together magically via a collective history of years of repetition. I read the card for "Helice's Potted Chicken" and wonder whose name should really be there—her mother Roslyn's, or her grandmother's before that?

In my house, some of these recipes define holidays. It would be a violation, heresy, to have a Jewish holiday meal without "Lila's Crunchy Jell-O Mold." Lila was my mother's best friend throughout my childhood and a good part of theirs. They grew up together in Brooklyn and were friends since high school. There was never a holiday that our families were not together—Thanksgiving, Rosh Hashanah, Fourth of July. I remember as a child, Lila teaching me how to say the prayer while lighting the Chanukah candles. I don't know which made me more proud—my memorized Hebrew or being able to strike a match. At some point during my college years, my mother and Lila ended their friendship for unclear reasons. I miss her, but my memory of Lila never fades. I always pause for a moment when I take out the recipe for "Lila's Crunchy Jell-O Mold," which continues to be a fixture at our holiday table.

My maternal grandmother, with whom I was very close, died 14 years ago. But I still have "Nanny's Chopped Liver." She wasn't a particularly talented cook and definitely not a zealous one. But there were a few things that she did make very well, among these, her chopped liver. She taught me how to make it when I was a teenager. Upon finally deeming my version acceptable, she happily announced that she would now, never have to make chopped liver again.

Some names have become part of my children's lexicon. My son regularly asks, "Are we having 'Marjorie's Salad' tonight?" He doesn't even know who Marjorie is. But I do. And I smile whenever I open the refrigerator and see the container of vinaigrette with her name written on the label.

A few, rare cards do not make me smile. I am often tempted to rewrite the card reading "Gail's Basic Stir-Fry Sauce," omitting her name, now that we've omitted each other from our lives. But I don't. She was a casualty of my divorce. The dissolution of my marriage demanded that she examine her own and that proved to be too painful. It was more comfortable to walk away from me. She was a better cook than friend. But there was a time when that was not the case; so her name lingers with the sharp bite of her sauce.

Not all the names are the remains of memories of people long-gone. Some are still quite present, my mother being one. She is an inspired cook, although one might suspect otherwise when reading the recipe for "Audrey's Fluffy Matzo Balls." There's a caveat at the bottom in her handwriting. After "Boil covered, 25 minute," it reads, "When done, throw away, and start again. They never come out right the first time."

I wonder in whose little black recipe boxes my name might appear, what stories come to mind when they happen upon the card for "Janie's Lentil Soup," whose children ask for "Janie's Fruit Crisp" without even knowing who Janie is.

I survey the cards in my recipe box and mull over the names—women and their food as part of my personal history. I hope that these names will stay alive forever. But for now, they're living in my kitchen. And tonight? It's "Lauren's Fruit Cobbler" for dessert!

Lila's Crunchy Jell-O Mold

Serves 8

Somehow it never feels like a holiday in our house unless this dish is on the table. I know it would make Lila happy to hear that a whole new generation of kids is demanding her Jell-O mold!

Two 3 oz. boxes black raspberry Jell-O
2 c. boiling water
1 c. cold water
1 apple, peeled, cored, and chopped
1 pear, peeled, cored, and chopped
4 oz. walnuts, chopped
2 stalks celery, chopped
8 oz. can crushed pineapple
16 oz. can whole cranberries

1. Place contents of Jell-O packets in large bowl. Add boiling water, stirring until Jell-O is completely dissolved. Stir in cold water. Refrigerate until thickened, about one-and-a-half hours.

2. Add other ingredients to bowl and mix. Pour into one-quart mold. (I prefer silicone because it is easier to unmold than metal.) Refrigerate until set (about two to three hours).
3. To unmold, place large serving plate on top of mold and quickly invert. Place dish towel soaked in hot water over mold for few minutes. Raise mold pan; Jell-O salad should slip out easily. Decorate with lettuce leaves or edible flowers, like pansies or nasturtiums, if in season.

FULL OF BEANS

Irene MacCollar

No event in our family was complete without baked beans. Through four generations—and a German shepherd with a poor digestive system—packing into Grandma's tiny dining room for Christmas dinner, to the church potluck, to the Fourth of July cookout all through the '60s, beans were to us symbolic of community and family. My grandmother fed the dog scraps constantly from the table. The damn dog would burp and fart, but we never knew if it was him or Grandma so no one ever made a comment.

You see, the women in my family (I'll refer to them as the Weeden Women), including four sisters, a sister-in-law, two grand-aunts, and the matriarch, Cora Weeden herself, each baked beans much differently from the other. Each woman presented her dish proudly. It was an unspoken rivalry, never openly discussed lest the subject become testy. The table was filled with beans—pushing other dishes, including traditional entrees and sides like roast turkey, baked ham and potatoes, to the edges as incidentals. It seemed normal to me then, but now I can see it was a bit excessive.

My mom's baked beans were heavy on molasses, and she used large, dark, thick-skinned specimens grown on our own land and dried on cookie sheets in massive quantities. She cut her salt pork into one- or two-inch dices. Her secret weapon was the pressure cooker, "to get all the gas out of the beans," although the strategy never worked. Mom was the worrying type, and banished all children from the kitchen, just in case the cooker exploded. For my childish imagination, the appliance made a perfect villain, violently shooting steam from its nostrils, ready to blow at any time. The envisioned carnage from "the Wrath of the Pressure Cooker" was delightfully morbid for a prepubescent writer who imagined dismembered bodies and a mixture of blood and beans sprayed on the walls.

Aunt Harriet's beans were soft and light brown with huge chunks of salt pork. She is one of the few original Weeden Women surviving. A few years back, she surprised me by traveling 225 miles by car from her home in upstate New York to Portland, Maine, and then another half hour by boat to my house on Peaks Island, all the while toting a wedding-sized batch of baked beans!

Aunt Bertha, if I remember right, baked beans off-white in color–white sugar and no molasses. She cut her salt pork in strips and distributed them evenly throughout.

As was tradition, immediately following the eating-of-the-beans, the men were banished to the great outdoors to smoke cigars, compare cars, and, most important, deal with the quick-acting gaseous effects of the beans—difficult to hold back. They could sit out there, talking, smoking, cursing, scratching, and farting all they wanted; it seemed a primitive camaraderie. The women didn't want them underfoot, neither while they were gossiping nor cleaning up.

Now, Bertha is gone; Grandma died in 1981 after burying both sisters, Dolly and Jessie. My mother is in hospice care, preparing to make her exit. My older sister died of cancer in the early 1990s. It has become the burden of my generation not only to pass on the legacy of the Weeden Women's beans, but to resurrect the sense of family that they symbolized.

Back in the "Days of The Beans," most of us lived within a half-mile of Grandma's house. These days the extended family is geographically scattered. It's now all but a physical impossibility for us to get together for Christmas or a summer cookout.

Although my sister and I have confessed to each other that we've experimented with "the beans" on occasion, I'm afraid we have failed miserably in maintaining the legacy. Someday I will teach my only child, a male gourmet cook, how to bake beans. Perhaps, he will in turn pass it down to the children and grandchildren I hope he will have.

Unfortunately, the memories will be lost. The new generation never knew so many of the players, re-telling stories never quite do them justice. Grandma in her favorite 1920's apron serving Christmas dinner; Aunts Dolly and Jessie—twins—snickering and giggling like little girls, their octogenarian eyes sparkling with love for each other and the family around them; all the men sitting in the yard together smoking pipes and cigars and gossiping like women; and last but not least, the newest Weeden baby, passed around the table, reducing even the toughest uncle to cooing and cuddles.

These things I will cherish until I, too, am gone.

Weeden Baked Beans

Serves at least 10

2 lbs. dried Great Northern beans
1 lg. yellow onion
12 oz. salt pork, leanest chunk you can find (which is not easy)
1 c. light brown sugar, packed
1 c. white sugar
⅛ c. molasses
1 T. yellow mustard
1 T. black pepper
No salt!

1. Place beans in colander. Run fingers through; cup beans, examining carefully for stones. It is not unusual to find some; many look just like beans. Wash beans well under cold running water.
2. In very large glass or Pyrex bowl, soak beans—unrefrigerated—overnight in water to cover by about two inches. They will absorb water and enlarge considerably; check occasionally to make sure there is enough water and room in container for them to expand.
3. The next day, discard soaking liquid. Place beans in large, heavy saucepan and cover again with water. Over medium heat, bring to a boil, continuing until skin peels when you blow on one bean. Continue boiling for another 30 minutes to an hour until fork tender.
4. Preheat oven to 375°F.
5. Slice onion vertically into fat slices. Place slices in bottom of large deep casserole or Dutch oven.
6. Cut salt pork into at least four pieces. Cut off any skin and most of fat, ending up with about three-fourths of original chunk. Cut pieces into one-and-one-half-inch cubes. Add cubes and sugars to casserole.
7. Drain off water from beans and discard. Then add beans to casserole.
8. Add molasses, mustard, and pepper. Stir well.
9. Add water to cover beans by about an inch or two.
10. Bake in preheated oven for about three hours, checking every half hour to make sure beans are just covered by water. Stir well every hour. Stop adding water when beans become very soft, and then cook only another half hour to an hour, checking to see that beans are juicy and not dried out. Remove from oven. Serve immediately, or allow to cool a bit.

BURNED SUGAR PIE: IT'S A SECRET

Traci Marie Nathans-Kelly

My family is not one of great intrigue. My dad tells the occasional story about my paternal grandfather's run-in with the Chicago mob in the 1920s when he was a small-town deputy. My maternal great-great grandfather was abandoned as a newborn on church steps in Ireland. We also had a bit of celebrity mixed in; my family knew Ernest Hemingway well during his Idaho days.

In recent years, however, there have been no mysteries . . . except, of course, Burned Sugar Pie. If anything haunts this family, it's that damn pie.

Growing up in Twin Falls, Idaho, my mother's table glowed on holidays with silver and china. Each woman of the family brought special dishes. Grammy Peg (my maternal grandmother) came with sugar cookies and mincemeat pies. Aunt Ruth was in charge of rolls. My paternal grandmother, Pearl, arrived with marshmallow salad and Burned Sugar Pie.

When I decided a decade ago to write some snippets of memoir, my thoughts went right to Burned Sugar Pie. Unfortunately, at the time, Pearl was in a full-care facility, preoccupied with feeding imaginary doves and awaiting phantom visits from John Wayne. She could no longer tell me the history of her pie. She wouldn't have anyway. The recipe is a secret . . . passed on only to the married women of the family. Each was, in turn, sworn to secrecy. Nothing I can recall, ever, brought forth more furtive glances and lowered voices than talk of Burned Sugar Pie.

According to Pearl, before her memory clouded, she told me of special pans and spoons that had to be used. Those secrets had not been committed to paper; they were part of her oral history. Since I needed a writing prompt, I called my mother, Mib, asking in a brave voice for the recipe. She hesitatingly agreed to send it to me. As she did, my father took the phone.

"Don't be givin' that out," he warned. "It's a secret. Ma don't want it bein' spread around."

"I wouldn't think of that, Dad," I said. "I just want to make it."

"Ya know," he continued, "that recipe is worth $25,000."

"Don't worry, Dad." I said.

I had seen many of Pearl's cards before; they were filled with small notes, dates, things crossed out. But when this recipe arrived by mail, I found something different. Piecing together clues, I figured out that the recipe was sent to my mom in 1966, right before Pearl's first big mother-in-law visit. But there were other intriguing bits. Here is the narrative that goes with the recipe (and, yes, some letters are missing; Pearl typed right off of the edge of the card!).

. *Burn sugar. The sugar, butter*
& water in fry pay and burn until it's darker than
Mikes hair. QUICK pour over first mixture and mix to-
gether. Pour in pie shell which has been bakes OR
a graham   cracker crust.   *Mom.*   *over*

Honey, this was given to me in 1935 by a friend. It
was with the understanding I'd never pass it on. I ga
it to Roma, showed her how to make it. I'd like for y
to know how. Mike and Larry are sooooo fond of it. I
use egg whites for meringue—-B U T the new Dream Whip
is very good now.
Maybe I can make one IF I fly in before Xmas of 1966.
Okay?
                                    Dec. 5, 1966
                                        Love Mom.

When Pearl writes that the mixture should be "darker than Mike's hair," she was referring to my father. But it was more than a recipe; it was a letter, a mini memoir, and a recipe all at once.

This was Burned Sugar Pie, and it was family history—Pearl, Mike, Larry, Roma, Mib.

When I was a child, Pearl told me that when I married, she would pass on the recipe. I wasn't married, but now I had the recipe in hand. Because I had acquired it without Pearl's knowledge, I felt I was betraying a trust while honoring her, too. I had decided that my story had to start with her recipe.

On January 8, 1995, Pearl died. While sorting through her things, my mother came across an old notebook full of hand-written recipes. She called me excitedly. "You won't believe this, but Burned Sugar Pie was something Pearl made up! The original recipe was called Caramel Pie."

Mib sent me Pearl's old Rock Island High School notebook. Caramel Pie was, indeed, copied into that book. Tucked in the notebook was the original postcard, dated 1943 on which Mrs. Lon Harding had originally penned the recipe.

Mrs. Harding's instructions are scant. There is no "Burn sugar" or "QUICK pour over first mixture" or anything about color. Most significantly, nowhere on the postcard does Mrs. Harding ask Pearl to keep the confidence. Apparently, the secrecy, the re-naming of the recipe, and detailed directions were entirely of Pearl's making.

In that notebook, Pearl had copied Burned Sugar Pie over and over, on different kinds of cards, different colors ink. All acknowledged Mrs. Harding. Repeatedly, Pearl noted, "I am the only person Mrs. H. ever gave this to. I don't pass the pie receipt out. Keep it for special company."

But Mrs. Harding's Caramel Pie became Pearl's Burned Sugar Pie. In the 1943 version, the word "caramel" has been zigzagged through with a blue ballpoint, and at a jaunty angle, "Burned Sugar" has been inserted. Pearl would think it more colorful to serve something called Burned Sugar Pie rather than Caramel Pie.

The recipe's transformation to an elaborate construction embracing family history and secrecy is fascinating to me. As Pearl evolved, so did the recipe. And now that I have inherited this treasure, Pearl's relationship with Mrs. Harding has faded; the story now belongs to the next generations.

I am still not willing to reveal Pearl's actual recipe even though I've seen it online. I feel it would be betraying a trust she had in me. Last night, my mom said that Pearl was "holding us hostage with that recipe." But I like the idea of a family secret that bonds the female members together.

As I nudge up against my fourth decade, I often get caught up in daily activities—like watching my toddler. A treasured moment with him was when he made a pretend pie, served it up, saying, "This is only for Henry and Mommy, only us." I have no doubt that he was channeling Pearl.

Burned Sugar Pie (not Pearl's, however!)

Serves ? Depends on how big you like your slices!

Filling

1 c. sugar, divided
2 T. flour
1 c. milk
2 eggs, separated
1 T. butter, unsalted
1 t. vanilla extract
One 9-inch pre-baked pie shell

1. In small saucepan over medium heat, combine one-half cup sugar, flour, milk, yolks, butter, and vanilla. Stir while heating until butter melts and mixture is smooth.

2. In second small saucepan, melt remaining one-half cup sugar over low heat until golden.
3. Slowly pour caramel into egg mixture. Continue cooking over low heat, stirring constantly until thick.
4. Pour filling into pie shell. Let set at room temperature or chill before topping with meringue.

Meringue

2 egg whites
¼ t. cream of tartar
3 T. sugar
¼ t. vanilla extract

1. Preheat oven to 300°F. With electric mixer on low, beat egg whites and cream of tartar for one minute until foamy and soft peaks form.
2. Add sugar one tablespoon at a time, and continue beating on high until stiff peaks form and sugar dissolves, about two minutes.
3. Beat in vanilla. Top pie with meringue, sealing to edges of crust.
4. Bake 12 to 15 minutes until lightly browned.

THANKSGIVING COMPROMISE—STUFFING AND DRESSING

Arlene Voski Avakian

We met the first day I took my son to his therapist in the town we moved to after I left my husband. The office was in the therapist's house and the "waiting room" was the kitchen, living room, or yard. The late September afternoon already had a hint of the glorious New England autumn light, and I sat outside while Neal was in his session. Within a few minutes, a Volkswagen van drove up and a woman with red hair, freckles, and a big smile came toward me with her hand out.

"Hi, I am Martha Ayres, the other therapist. I am going to have some coffee. Would you like some? It will only take a minute."

True to her word, she came back very quickly, and as she approached me, I recognized the odor of instant coffee. She took a sip, smacked her lips, and sat down. I wondered what kind of person actually liked instant coffee, but as we began to talk and I felt her openness and warmth, I took a sip of the coffee and thought it might be drinkable. Each week as I drove up the driveway, I hoped Martha would be there and miraculously, she always was. The hour had become an oasis for me in a very dry year—my first as a single parent and graduate student trying desperately to be the superwoman the women's liberation movement convinced us we could be. By the spring I wanted to see Martha for more than an hour a week. I invited her for dinner again and again, and finally realized with a bit of a shock that I had fallen in love.

What drew us together was what we shared, but we quickly learned about our differences. Martha is from a very small town in West Virginia, and I grew up in New York City. Both sides of her family came to the United States many generations ago from England and Scotland; my maternal relatives were refugees from the Armenian genocide in Turkey, and my father's family, also Armenian, were in diasporas in Iran before they emigrated to the United States.

My take on the world is material, economic, and political, while hers is psychological and spiritual. I am an atheist. She believes in God. She has always been a lesbian. I had never been with a woman before. I had two children. She never wanted children. She was close to her family. I was alienated from mine.

Some of these differences were funny, even endearing, but others felt so intractable that we hated them—and sometimes each other—for the threat they posed to our relationship. We were often taken aback by the suddenness of our clashes. We could be in the midst of a seemingly neutral or even pleasant interaction when one of us would set off an intense reaction in the other by a mistaken assumption of commonality. While we learned to approach each other more carefully and became adept at dealing with the eruptions, some topics continued to be emotional land mines. Thanksgiving dinner was one.

When I was very young, my immigrant family didn't celebrate Thanksgiving. We used this American day off to gather for a sumptuous meal of roast lamb, Persian pilaf, and okra or string beans stewed in tomato sauce, flavored with onions, garlic, olive oil, basil, tarragon, and oregano. Sometimes we had roast chicken, but it was never stuffed with anything, nor was it surrounded by a sweet potato casserole topped with little marshmallows, creamed onions, and cranberry sauce. When I approached my teens and began my campaign to become a real "American," I knew I had to change my family as well as myself, and one component was fashioning a real Thanksgiving dinner. My mother complied with turkey and cranberry sauce, but not any of the other accoutrements. During the 1960s I had learned through the American Indian Movement that Thanksgiving was a celebration of the genocide perpetrated by the United States government on the indigenous people, so I had ceased to celebrate. But it *was* a day off and, happy for any excuse to prepare feasts, I cooked wonderful meals for my husband, children, and friends, but never turkey and trimmings.

Martha's large paternal family gathered at her grandparents' home. Her beloved Mamaw prepared all the dishes: mashed potatoes, stuffing and dressing, homemade cranberry sauce, yeast rolls, pumpkin, apple, and mincemeat pies. She genuinely missed being with her family on holidays, especially for Thanksgiving dinner.

In addition to all my other problems with Thanksgiving, I could not relate to the cuisine. My food basics are basil, tarragon, parsley, oregano, olive oil, butter, garlic, cumin, rice, lamb, tomatoes, eggplant, string beans, okra, phyllo, and walnuts. My culinary and ethnic judgment of this meal was that it represented the epitome of WASP food.

Our early Thanksgivings together were treasured because the children went to their father's for the four-day weekend and we spent the precious time luxuriating in each other and oblivious to anything else. When the children no longer went away on Thanksgiving, we began our negotiations about what to do for the holiday Martha looked forward to and I dreaded. We invited friends. We had potlucks. Sometimes I even had fun, but we almost always had a fight before, during, and/or after the big day.

As the main cook in our family, I made the turkey and some of the trimmings—no marshmallows—but I relished neither the meal nor the day. Martha made the stuffing. One year, I found a recipe for rice pilaf stuffing. I carefully approached Martha with the idea of trying a new stuffing. She looked at me suspiciously and asked, "What about my grandmother's stuffing?" I remembered that she had talked about dressing—stuffing outside of the bird—and suggested that she do that and I would stuff the turkey with the wonderful Middle Eastern mixture. She agreed to try it. We both loved the dressing and stuffing, and since then we have a very harmonious Thanksgiving, which we begin by paying our respects to Native Americans.

Martha's Dressing

Serves 8

Two 1 lb. bags of bread stuffing, herbed and corn
2 c. chopped celery
2 c. diced onions
2 T. (or more) poultry seasoning, sage, thyme
2 eggs, lightly beaten
4 c. turkey broth
1 c. turkey drippings or butter
Salt and pepper

1. Preheat oven to 350°F.
2. Mix all ingredients. Be sure to smell mixture for seasoning. Don't taste because of raw eggs, but your nose is a great guide. You should be able to smell sage and thyme. If you can't, add more. Put dressing into large open pan and bake for an hour. Serve immediately.

Arlene's Stuffing

Makes enough for 15-to 20lb. turkey

1 lb. sausage
4 T. butter
½ c. diced onion
½ c. pine nuts
1 ½ c. long grain white rice (basmati is best)
½ c. currants
3 c. chicken broth
¼ t. cinnamon
¼ t. allspice
½ c. finely chopped Italian parsley
Salt and pepper

1. Preheat oven to 350°F.
2. Wash basmati rice in cold water until water runs clear. Drain.
3. Toast pine nuts in oven until lightly browned.
4. Cook sausage in frying pan over medium heat until it loses red color. Drain on paper towels. When cool, crumble.
5. Melt butter in heavy pot with tight lid, and sauté onions over medium heat until translucent. Add rice and stir until each grain is coated with butter. Add pine nuts, currants, parsley, cinnamon, allspice, and sausage. Stir for one minute and add chicken broth. Bring to boil. Add salt and pepper to taste.
6. Turn down heat to low, and cook for 25 minutes. When stuffing is done, fluff with fork and leave uncovered until ready to stuff turkey.

CHICKEN À L'ORANGE

Ellen Perry Berkeley

I chuckle every time I think of Chicken *à l'Orange*. Nothing spells culinary sophistication like a dish with a French name. I suppose it should be called *Poulet à l'Orange* for maximum effect, a name that conjures up pristine white chicken breast, gently sautéed in white wine, amid orange wedges and a dash of Grand Marnier (or so I'm told–I'm not a fancy cook, myself).

The source of the orange in my recipe, however, is simply frozen orange juice, and the preparation is almost ludicrous–only two ingredients and only four minutes prep time (well, maybe six, if you're distracted by TV, guests, or cocktails). This is the standard dish I use for entertaining. Time after time, I've announced its name with an inner chortle. Guests are always impressed, both by the pretentious name as well as the tasty dish.

Whenever I'm asked where the recipe comes from, I have no good answer. I once thought it came from my sister-in-law, but she denies any knowledge of it. I dimly recall seeing it in the *New York Times*, but the *Times* would probably disavow any association.

I've made this dish for several decades now, so any detective work would be difficult. Then, too, I've never purchased the newest cookbooks, or followed TV cooking shows, so any attempt to link the recipe to the latest fad would be similarly unproductive.

Grasping at a final straw, I've wondered whether the entrée came from my mother. Born just as the 19th century became the 20th, she felt obliged to become a serious artist–in any medium except food. (She was an accomplished ceramist.) Chicken *à l'Orange* is not among the few simple recipes I inherited from her. Until I wrote down the directions for this essay, in fact, the details existed only in my memory.

But my memory is rich in associations. The person I think of most lovingly in connection with this fail-safe formula is my dear cousin Joan, to whom I passed it along. She cooked it for her two sons so often that they jokingly threatened to leave home. Her guests ate it repeatedly, loving her for it–more, perhaps, than they loved the dish itself.

Joan, who died recently–at the young age of 73–was one of my dearest friends. We didn't know each other well as children. We lived just a few towns apart, but our families were not close. Then, before I turned ten, her family moved to Arizona, to relieve her father's severe arthritis.

We met again as young wives in California. Her then-husband was teaching in the sociology department at Stanford University. I was also living in Palo Alto, working in an architect's office while my then-husband was employed by a city planning office several towns to the south. When Joan and her husband discovered that they could build a home on the Stanford campus in a new faculty housing development, they turned to me. I had done graduate work in architecture. Without a license, I couldn't call myself an "architect." But as an "architectural designer," I could be the sole and official creator of a single-family residence. Joan and I spent many delightful hours developing an interesting and workable home for her. I don't recall that we ate Chicken *à l'Orange* then, but perhaps we did. I do remember that her kitchen was intentionally minimal. She wasn't keen on cooking. (A later resident in the house, a highly celebrated–but unreadable–philosopher, seems also to have loved the house; he probably wasn't keen on cooking either.)

For many years, Joan and I were living far from each other. Then each of us went through a divorce, and both of us were soon on the East Coast. Now we could meet more regularly, and these were close times. On one of her visits from Philadelphia to New York, I made us Grandma's borscht. We were each going through difficult times. I was remarried, and struggling with fertility procedures. Joan was struggling with raising two young sons as a single mother. As we sipped the cold soup on that troubling day, we remembered our grandmother and her own difficulties–she had come to the United States in the 1880s, married a man who was decent but not loving, and never again saw the sweetheart she had left behind in Czarist Russia. But she maintained a gracious and optimistic nature, despite her situation, and we vowed to emulate her.

As a result of our lovely connection on that afternoon, I later developed my book *At Grandmother's Table*. No, Joan wasn't a contributor to this homage to the grandmother-granddaughter connection, but she exulted with me when it earned high praise, and when it reached the top 100 in sales on Amazon.com. And she enjoyed considering it, with me, a book of history– women's history, American history, culinary history, cultural history–rather than a cookbook. (As I mentioned, I'm not much of a cook.)

In 1999, when my second husband suggested that we take Joan with us to London the year after her second husband died, we rented a "self-catering flat" and cooked Chicken *à l'Orange* at least once—for fun, and for relief from our elegant restaurant meals. Joan told me later that this trip had restored her to life, after her time of mourning. I'd like to believe that Chicken *à l'Orange* was important in her recovery.

By this time she died at the premature age of 73, Joan had become a noted criminologist; her lengthy obituary appeared in the *New York Times*. She was a whiz at anything intellectual but a total loss in the kitchen. Several of us laughed gently at her funeral, thinking how this simple recipe had given the world so many more hours of her mind.

I hope it will do the same for you and will provide many good times with friends and family. To me, this dish will always bring back wonderful memories of Joan. I wouldn't hazard a guess as to how often she made it, but it always brought a smile to each of us as we prepared and served it.

Chicken *à l'Orange*

1 lb. chicken parts (breasts, thighs, wings) for 2 to 3 people; 2 lb. for 4 to 6
   people; more if you want leftovers)
One to two 12 oz. cans frozen orange juice, depending on quantity of chicken

1. Preheat oven to 350–375°F.
2. Wash chicken pieces and arrange on foil-lined baking pan.
3. Spoon orange juice over chicken.
4. Bake for 45 minutes, turning pieces several times and basting them with
   melted orange juice.
5. Remove chicken from pan. Allow orange juice to cook 10 minutes longer,
   until it darkens fetchingly.
6. Return chicken to pan for few minutes, to reheat. Don't allow chicken to
   overcook, or it will be dried out and unchewable, making conversation
   difficult.
7. Serve–perhaps with something classy, like wild rice–to shouts of delight
   and requests for this recipe that (in everyone's opinion) has kept you over
   a hot stove for hours!

GINGERBREAD MEMORIES

Rebecca Libourel Diamond

The year my aunt and I started making gingerbread houses together was
a painful time. Her daughter, my cousin, had passed away only the month
before, and we were both still stinging from the shock.

The gingerbread house played an important role in our shared grief. The
recipe came from a Swedish friend of my aunt, who had given one of these
magical creations to my cousin as a child, and my aunt had made several
over the years. I had always been interested and figured the time was right
to give it a try, so we set a date for late November.

My cousin's spirit was with us that day. She and I had been very close
growing up in New Jersey; although we grew apart during adolescence, I
always cared about her deeply. She was an only child and while she loved
all her extended family, she and I had a special bond. We were the same
age and more like best friends than cousins, even with our contrasting
personalities. I am more serious and love to read and write, whereas she
was fun-loving and creative.

As a teenager, my cousin started using drugs and alcohol, which ulti-
mately caused her death. During the times she was addicted, my feelings

Rebecca Diamond and her aunt Nancy Prince with the 10th annual ginger-bread house they made together for Christmas 2009. © Rebecca Libourel Diamond. Used by permission.

for her ranged from sadness and disappointment to pity and anger. It was so hard to see this happen to someone I had known as a different person.

That afternoon my aunt and I both welcomed the chance to reflect on my cousin and her life. In between rolling out warm, fragrant dough, waiting for it to bake, and then decorating the pieces, we shared thoughts and memories, gaining deeper insight into the young woman who had meant so much to many people.

It turned out to be a very healing experience, so we decided to meet again the following year, and then the next, at which point we realized the baking had become an annual event. My two children, Cate and Patrick, are now included in the fun and eagerly anticipate the occasion. They adore my aunt and she is very kind and patient with them. Cate even wrote about making the gingerbread house as her favorite holiday custom for a school project.

There have been years when I was busy attending to one of the children while my aunt did most of the work. One year, she and Cate made the house while I soothed poor Patrick, who was ill. Then we lived in England for two years. While there, the kids and I built the house solo one year, but my aunt was visiting for the other so were able to keep the tradition going.

Baking with my aunt has been a wonderful learning experience. Much of what is involved in the construction of the gingerbread house was new to me. I was surprised to see that the dough is rolled out while still warm. It has such a nice feel and smells more fragrant than dough that has been chilled.

Once the pieces are baked and cooled, the next step is decorating with white icing. I had never before used a pastry bag and my aunt still patiently assists me every year (her deft fingers wield it perfectly).

The actual assembling comes next and this is not easy! My aunt expertly spreads the icing mortar along the edges and corners and firmly holds them in place while they dry. It really helps to have two people perform this tricky maneuver. Once the wall pieces are attached, the roof is placed on top. If it is too heavy, it slides off–a fact I learned from experience. The chimney is constructed separately and then gently "glued" on when the house is sturdy enough. For final touches, we bake extra dough into gingerbread figures that are placed outside the house, a reindeer on the roof and a "welcome" sign etched with our last name out front.

One thing I've always liked about this house is its modest design–simple hearts, curlicues, and flowers drawn with white icing, and then a dusting of powdered sugar to simulate snow. However, it is a slow process. Spending all this time with my aunt has made me realize that cooking with a companion can be a very therapeutic activity. I look forward to our yearly baking as much for the conversation as the product. My aunt has shared memories of growing up, and we've discussed everything from religion and politics to child-rearing, books, and, of course, cooking. We always make sure to include recollections of my cousin. This year will mark the tenth anniversary of her passing, and ten gingerbread houses.

Pepparkakshus (Gingerbread House)

Make pattern out of cardboard for following pieces:

- Two rectangles (three by seven inches) for end pieces of house with peaks (center point should be few inches higher than top of walls) to give roof its top line. Cut out windows.
- Two rectangles (four by eight inches) for roof.
- Two rectangles (four by five inches) for front and back of house. Cut out door and windows.
- Four pieces for chimney (one by three inches, one by two inches, and two pieces one by three inches on one side and one by two inches on opposite (so base is angled to fit roof line).

Dough

1 c. butter
1 c. brown sugar, firmly packed
1 c. molasses
5 c. sifted flour
1 T. baking soda
1 T. cinnamon
1 T. ground ginger

1. Preheat oven to 375°F.
2. In large saucepan over low heat, melt butter, then add brown sugar and molasses, stirring frequently until well blended.
3. Sift together flour, baking soda, cinnamon, and ginger. Stir into warm molasses mixture.
4. While dough is still warm, take about one quarter and shape into ball. Roll out on lightly floured surface to rectangle about one-eighth-inch thick. (First ball will produce a front and side piece, and perhaps a piece or two of chimney.) Make sure to cut out door and window from front piece and windows from side pieces. Reserve door for baking since it will be used later.
5. Place pieces on parchment paper-lined baking sheets and bake five to eight minutes until edges barely begin to brown and surface is no longer puffy. Using sharp paring knife, trim pieces that have expanded during baking, using pattern pieces as guides, then return to oven for about two more minutes.
6. Remove baking sheets carefully to wire racks to cool.
7. Repeat with remaining dough until all pieces of house are cut out.

Icing

1 egg white
2 c. sifted confectioners' sugar
1 t. lemon juice

1. Beat ingredients together with mixer at high speed until firm. Icing should be soft enough to flow through fine pastry tube, but stiff enough to hold shape. While mixing, add few drops lemon juice or one teaspoon water to thin down consistency. Spoon into pastry bag and carefully pipe outlines of shingles, door, and window trim, and any other details you like. Use icing as mortar to glue together various pieces.
2. Place finished, assembled house on white cardboard covered with aluminum foil. Sift confectioners' sugar over house to simulate snow.

COOKIES

Lisa Heldke

My family takes its cookies seriously. Other people might regard a cookie as a second-class dessert, a poor substitute for pie or cake, or something really significant, like a torte or bombe. Not the Heldkes. For us, when push comes to dessert, we'd just as soon have a cookie. A homemade cookie, that is, made, preferably, by a blood relative—or at least someone whose membership in the family is of long enough standing that they know the Four Great Truths of cookie baking:

- It Doesn't Matter If The Recipe Says Vegetable Shortening; Use Butter.
- Just Because Bakeries Underbake Things Is No Reason For Us To Do So.
- Don't Be Chintzy. If It Says A Cup, Use A Heap.
- Those Putzy Cookies Made From Dough Dyed Some Godawful Color, and Decorated With Those Silver Balls That Will Break Your Teeth Are Never Any Good Anyway, So Why Go To All The Work Of Making Them In The First Place?

Our family cookie jar in Rice Lake, Wisconsin, (in truth, an ice bucket my parents got as a wedding present) was never empty. During the everyday cookie season (January through November), it was stocked with chocolate chip (semi-sweet chocolate, walnuts, and coconut), peanut butter (Skippy Super Chunk), ginger snap (my mother's choice; she makes a sandwich using two snaps and a piece of sharp cheddar cheese), or oatmeal raisin. ("Dad's favorite" we call 'em. Why do people insist on putting cinnamon in oatmeal cookies????)

During High Cookie Season (also known as Christmastime), no single cookie jar could accommodate our creations; we filled the freezer with peanut blossoms, Russian tea cakes, candy bar cookies, rum balls. But even our holiday baking adheres to the Great Truths—including #4. No fussy cutout gingerbread men or dainty hand-molded mice for us.

The one exception to our Keep It Simple rule was the Chocolate Peanut Butter Pinwheel, the cookie that broke our hearts year after year. It sounds simple enough: roll out a thin slab of peanut butter dough, slather it with melted chocolate chips, roll it up jelly roll fashion, refrigerate 'til firm, slice, and bake. What could be hard about that?

Well, as it turns out, everything. Complications arise the minute you roll out the dough. It must be soft enough to roll, but not too soft, or when you spread the melted chocolate, it will turn to mush. Solution: roll out dough, slam it in the freezer 'til it firms up, and then spread with melted chocolate.

But wait! Don't leave it in the freezer too long! If you do, the dough will get so cold that, when you spread the melted chocolate, it will immediately harden, and you'll never be able to make the jelly roll. (Can I just say that my stomach is tightening up even as I write this? The Cookie Season is upon us as I type, and I am more than a bit nervous about this year's pinwheels.)

If you manage to make it as far as the jelly roll stage without throwing the mess away, your troubles aren't over. When you put the now-rolled log of dough into the fridge to firm up, it should hold its circular profile. But it won't; it'll sag into a lopsided oval. Every pinwheel ever produced in my family's kitchen was an oval—that is, until the year my Jewish boyfriend showed up to help. His pinwheels were perfect circles, every one of them. Go figure.

But wait! There's more! You still have to slice these little devils! Here, if the dough is too soft and the chocolate too hard, the chocolate will shatter, leaving you with cookies that ought to be called "gravel driveway" or "dog's breakfast."

If you somehow surmount all these obstacles, then you'll probably put the cookies too close to each other on the cookie sheet and they'll grow together into one giant pinwheel blob. Or you'll forget to set the timer, and they'll burn to a crisp (beyond even the limits allowed by Rule #2). Yes, I'm speaking from experience here. Pinwheels have been breaking my heart for decades now.

My mother eventually just gave up on them, insisting that other peanut-butter-and-chocolate cookies taste "just the same." (I notice she never turns me down when I offer to bring her a bag of them from my stock, however!) I recently wrote Mom, to ask where this infernal recipe had come from. She searched her cookbooks, wracked her brain, scoured the house for clues . . . and came up with nothing. No idea. No inkling. This recipe came out of nowhere, set up housekeeping in the Heldke family home, and has not left us in peace ever since.

My sister vows she's going to make them this season. I hope she's laid in the Valium.

Chocolate Peanut Butter Pinwheels

Serves ? I get a different number every year, so I'm not saying.

½ c. unsalted butter, softened
1 c. sugar
½ c. peanut butter
1 egg
2 T. milk

1 ¼ c. flour
½ t. salt
1 t. baking soda
6 oz. semi-sweet chocolate chips

1. With electric mixer on medium, cream together butter, peanut butter, and sugar until fluffy. Add egg and milk; beat just to incorporate.
2. Add flour, soda, and salt, and beat on low just until fully incorporated.
3. Wrap dough in plastic wrap and chill in refrigerator for about an hour or so for easier handling. (Ha!)
4. Divide dough in half. Roll each half between sheets of wax paper, into a rectangle, one-quarter-inch thick. (I don't know how big a rectangle; just keep rolling until dough is a quarter of an inch thick. If you want lots of little pinwheels, make the rectangle long and narrow. If you want fewer bigger pinwheels, make your rectangle short and fat.)
5. Melt chips. (I use a double boiler because I manage to burn them in the microwave. If you're more attentive than I, feel free to use the microwave method.) Spread half over surface of each rectangle.
6. Roll up each rectangle, jelly roll fashion. Refrigerate half an hour.
7. While chilling rolls, preheat oven to 375°F.
8. Slice one-quarter- to one-half-inch thick slices. Place them two inches apart on cookie sheets.
9. Bake for eight to ten minutes or until just browned around edges. Or bake until deep brown all the way through, which is the way we Heldkes would do it. Suit yourself.
10. Cool cookies on dish towels placed on wire racks.

Food is the adhesive at the center of many of our relationships, unifying and connecting us in a very special bond. It helps develop important aspects of who we are.

6

Coming into Our Own

Recipes are not inviolable texts. They are guidelines, they are starting points.
Take them into the kitchen and make them your own.[1]

—Teresa Lust, *Pass the Polenta*

Some of our storied dishes evolve to a point where we launch new narratives, our own scripts. We may use an inherited template as a point of departure, but our own elaborations transforms the dish into something that is truly our own. This is an exhilarating experience, I think, with a sense of completeness and freedom. As part of coming into our own, we recognize and accept who we are and go public with these selves—our true identities. We may decide to risk everything, and rather than keep a family heirloom under wraps make the bold decision to share it with the world, as one writer did. Another felt liberated when she was finally able to master a mother's signature recipe so well that others assumed her mother had made it. Sometimes our emerging self-awareness comes from inventing our own traditions to suit ourselves and lifestyles. Now we know who we are.

OUR LADY, QUEEN OF *PIEROGI*

Kelly Jeske

On summer mornings as a child in Linwood, Michigan, I followed my Gram into her bedroom, as she got ready for the day. I always asked to play with the Virgin Mary statue that sat atop her mahogany dresser. Climbing onto the plush quilt, I cradled Mary between my hands, tracing the folds of her glass robe up to her compassionate face. I saw her as a protectress, beacon, and resting place. I felt calm and soothed; I felt understood and adored when with my Gram.

My grandmother is an artist, mother, grandmother, aunt, sister, and friend to many. She is a seeker and a revolutionary thinker. She wears gold sneakers to potlucks, leaves treats for her mail carrier, gives art lessons to children. I've always considered her a kindred spirit—we look deeply at one another and celebrate what we see.

As a first generation American, Gram carries many Polish traditions into her daily life. When my Papa was alive and they lived together in their cozy Michigan home, they had a "Polish room" filled with art and relics from family. As is true for many Polish people, the Blessed Mother is dear to Gram's heart. In Poland, Mary is Our Lady, Queen of Poland. I remember Gram sharing communion wafers sent by mail from relatives in Poland—square sheets imprinted with Polish words and symbols, sent as special blessings. Gram learned to play the accordion as a child, and still enjoys making music. Every night, Gram turns on a recording of her favorite polkas and dances in her kitchen.

Gram nourishes the world with her paintings, her accordion, her love, and her Polish cooking. The Blessed Mother nourishes the spirit; good food nourishes the body. Keeping with her parents' custom, Gram has always grown some of her own food—vegetables, herbs. Summers spent with my grandparents were filled with strawberries eaten warm from the midday sun, lettuce plucked straight from the garden and served with sweet and sour cream over new boiled potatoes, fresh eggs soft-boiled and eaten with butter, salt and pepper. Holidays brought fresh kielbasa from a local butcher, homemade *pierogi* with cabbage or potatoes and cheese, sweet and sour boiled cabbage, apple cake with caramel frosting, and fresh-baked bread. As I grew up, Gram taught me to make bread, showing me how to knead dough in her sunny yellow kitchen with the hand-painted strawberry border.

When I was 17, my 1986 off-white Ford Escort was the only place that felt entirely my own. After agonizing for months, I'd chosen to come out to Gram as lesbian. I asked her to go for a drive. I watched as Gram bent and folded into the passenger seat, her body closing into itself like an ornate paper fan. She was dressed in paint-splattered cotton shorts and a bright violet T-shirt with the resolution "When I Am an Old Woman, I Shall Wear Purple."

I pulled slowly out of the driveway. Squinting against the sun, I maneuvered the spaghetti-like curves of South Long Lake Road as Gram described the way the sunlight streaked through the leaves like a strobe light. As she talked, my mind swirled with trepidation. Am I really going to tell her? What if she just can't understand? After driving about five miles, I pulled into a parking lot and turned off the engine. Gripping the steering wheel, I drew in my breath and said, "Gram? I have something to tell you."

She looked at me cheerfully and smiled, cocking her head. The muscles in my shoulders contracted. I trembled like the leaves scattering across the windshield. "Gram, I want to tell you this because I love you . . . and because I want to be honest with you. Because I want you to really know me . . . I'm a lesbian!" I blurted.

She turned to me quizzically and her face softened. I was afraid she might cry until a gentle smile crept onto her lips.

"Well," she said slowly, "I always knew that I'd given you over to Her care." Grandma locked her eyes with mine and patted my leg for emphasis as she continued. "When you were born three months early and everyone was so sure you would die, well, I went to the hospital and prayed over your incubator and I asked the Blessed Mother to watch over you. And right at that moment you looked up at me with those big, brown eyes." She stopped to dab tears gathering in corners of her eyes and sighed deeply, "And I knew right then that you would live. I gave you over to feminine influence, to Mary. So, it makes sense to me that you love women."

I was astounded. I still am. In the early 1990s, my Polish-American, Catholic grandmother took my coming out in stride. In fact, she made sense of my identity through the lens of her faith—a faith with a doctrine that condemns homosexuality. My Gram, with her prayers to the Virgin, understood.

Nearly a decade later, my Gram came to visit me in Portland for the first time. She'd known my partner Meg for several years and she always treasured the opportunity to spend time with us. Gram looked at Meg and me, measured our love, and pronounced us family. Gram often talked about her thankfulness for Meg's presence in my life and she relished this chance to tangibly express her gratitude: she wanted to make special *pierogi*. We wandered through the grocery store, choosing smooth, gleaming red-skinned potatoes and flour. Gram scoured the cheese selection and settled on dill havarti. "She'll like this," Gram said, "This is special cheese." At home, Gram peeled, chopped, and boiled potatoes; mixed dough; cut small cubes of cheese. Chopping, mashing, and frying, filling and folding; Gram handcrafted *pierogi* like her mother. Reigning over our kitchen, she was the queen of *pierogi*. When there was a small pile of crisply browned pillows, Gram served platefuls to Meg and I. We relished this homemade

Polish food—a recipe handed down, prepared by my beloved Gram, and made sacred with her love. I was sure I could feel the Virgin Mary's smile; I imagined her blessing our family as we shared our meal.

Gram's *Pierogi*

Batter

2 eggs
¼ c. olive oil
1 c. milk
¼ c. sugar
2 c. flour, preferably whole wheat

1. In medium bowl, combine ingredients and blend to pancake batter consistency, using a bit more or less milk as needed.

Filling

1 lb. red potatoes, peeled, chopped into small pieces, boiled until tender, and drained
Dill Havarti cheese, cubed
Vegetable oil

1. While drained potatoes are still hot, mash together with cheese. Set aside.
2. In small skillet over medium-low heat, warm two tablespoons oil. Pour small circle of batter into pan and fry until browned. Flip over. Spoon dollop of potato-cheese filling onto one half of circle. When crepe is browned on second side, fold over to seal. Continue frying and filling until finished. Enjoy!

PIECRUST WITH SOUL

Sharon L. Jansen

At times I blame piecrust for my failed marriage. I know it's not true: bad pastry wasn't the reason everything went wrong. But. . . .

Shortly after I married in Seattle, my mother-in-law handed over Thanksgiving and Christmas dinners to me. I was thrilled. That meant baking pies, and the crust didn't go well. My first effort produced dry, crumbly dough. I had to press chunks into the pie plate, smoothing lumps and sealing cracks the best I could. But the pumpkin filling seeped out underneath anyway and burned the bottom of the pan.

The next time, the dough was so gooey, it stuck to the rolling pin. When I scraped off enough for the lattice top, the decoration looked like worms crawling across the mincemeat.

Over the years, my marriage and my piecrust went from bad to worse, and I began dreading the holidays. I started worrying in October, then in August, then on my birthday in July. No one told me to forget about pie and make a German chocolate cake—or fudgy, pecan-filled brownies or golden-topped crème brûlée. For whatever reason, I couldn't forget about pie either. I look back now and wonder who that woman was, that woman who thought perfect pastry would solve everything.

My failures made me a little frantic. I tried recipe after recipe. There was one that included hot water and shortening, another cold milk and oil, still a third contained vinegar, and then there was a flour-and-water paste version. I tried making pastry with butter, then lard. Another formula included egg and still others featured cream cheese, sour cream, and buttermilk, respectively. I tried weighing the flour instead of measuring it; I pulsed the dough in the food processor, I chilled it overnight.

I could have written a book. I *should* have written a book—but who would buy a cookbook about how *not* to make piecrust? A book filled with recipes for failure?

In desperation, I appealed to my mother for help. For once she made no comment about my request, just said that she felt like making lemon meringue pie one day and I could come watch her. Only when seated at her kitchen table, ready to take detailed notes, did I realize she didn't measure ingredients—just threw things together until her dough "felt right." A few deft strokes with a rolling pin and her translucent pastry shell slid obligingly into the waiting pie plate.

There was no way I could replicate it. In the end, I resorted to buying frozen pie shells at Albertson's supermarket. I sneaked them home, hid them in the back of the refrigerator to defrost, waited until I was alone to pry them out of their aluminum tins, and then laid them carefully in my own pans and re-crimped the edges. As for the disposable tin pans, I buried them in garbage cans behind the garage. The piecrust was horrible. No one else noticed.

After I left my marriage, I thought my piecrust problem had ended; I resolved never to make it again. As it turned out, I *did* leave my piecrust problem behind, but not in the way I thought. One summer day just a few months after I was divorced, I picked a bucket of blueberries and suddenly felt like making pie. My piecrust came together beautifully, rolled out perfectly, and that was that. It didn't take any special ingredient or technique, just the basic recipe in my battered copy of *The Joy of Cooking*.

On occasion, I remember my mother muttering during that long-ago tutorial something about piecrust and "the state of your soul." I had been too busy trying to take notes to pay much attention.

Now I am paying attention. When I sat down at my laptop to write this piece, I asked my mother for help. She sent along her recipe for lemon meringue pie.

Mom's Lemon Meringue Pie

Serves 8

I don't know where my mother got this recipe, but she has always loved lemon meringue pie, and this has been her favorite version for as long as I can remember. This is the pie she made when I asked for a piecrust tutorial. The recipe calls for a baked, cooled piecrust. Any piecrust will do if you know how to make it. Otherwise, I recommend the formula in The Joy of Cooking.

1 baked, cooled pie shell

Filling

3 eggs, separated (use whites for meringue)
2 t. grated lemon zest
⅓ c. fresh lemon juice (2 to 3 lemons)
1 c. sugar
4 T. cornstarch
¼ t. salt
1 ½ c. boiling water
2 T. unsalted butter

1. In medium bowl, stir together yolks, lemon zest, and juice. Set aside.
2. In medium saucepan, mix together sugar, cornstarch, and salt. Gradually stir in boiling water. Bring mixture to boil over medium heat, stirring constantly. Continue to boil and stir until mixture is clear and smoothly thickened, about three minutes.
3. Very slowly, add one-third cup hot mixture to yolks-and-lemon combination to temper eggs (so they won't scramble) and stir.

4. When egg-and-lemon mixture is warm, slowly add remainder of hot mixture, stirring well. Return combined mixture to saucepan and bring to boil again, cooking and stirring for about two minutes more.
5. Remove filling from heat and stir in butter. Allow filling to cool five minutes, pour into pie shell, and top with meringue.

Mom's "Magic" Meringue

This recipe is a relatively new addition to my mom's favorite pie. Before she acquired this formula, she made a more conventional version (egg whites, cold water, a little sugar) but always fretted about its tendency to "weep." While working as a cook in a school kitchen in the 1980s, she acquired this recipe that was circulating among the elementary school "cafeteria ladies." I don't know why she calls it "magic," but it certainly produces a very puffy and impressive topping, one that is very stable rather than touchy—thus the "magic."

3 egg whites
3 T. ice water
1 t. baking powder
6 T. sugar

1. Preheat oven to 400°F.
2. With electric mixer on low, beat egg whites in pristine clean bowl to light peaks, then add ice water and baking powder, beating on high until very stiff—you will know they have reached the right point when inserted fork can stand alone in the meringue. Add sugar slowly, one tablespoon at a time, beating constantly.
3. When sugar is completely incorporated, meringue is ready to spread over lemon filling, sealing all edges around pie shell.
4. Bake for six to eight minutes, just until meringue turns golden. Be sure to watch carefully so meringue does not burn.

A DESSERT, A GRADUATION, AND A WEDDING

Ammini Ramachandran

There was an aura of mystique around my mom's fabulous desserts, especially her *laddu*. Her sweets were not everyday fare; they were reserved for special occasions. She made *laddu* once a year at our home in Kerala, India, for *Navarathri* festival, the nine-night colorful Hindu celebration, and then again for family weddings. Small beads of deep-fried *besan* (chickpea) flour batter soaked in golden sugar syrup, and carefully shaped into small balls by her loving hands, were the most scrumptious treat.

Honestly, I did not realize how very special her *laddu* was until I moved to the United States. Mom taught me to cook through recipes she sent every week in her letters. When it came to measurements, she used a lot of "handfuls" and "pinches." They all worked after a couple of trials. But it took me over 15 years to muster the courage to try *laddu*. My first trial was a disaster. The sugar syrup turned brittle by the time I fried the *besan* beads. On a second attempt, I overcompensated, and the syrup became too watery and the *laddu* didn't hold their shape. I bought a candy thermometer to gauge the right syrup consistency, another to measure the heat of the ghee (clarified butter) in which the batter is fried, and measuring cups to calculate amounts properly. Finally, after several trials and errors, I managed to make decent *laddu*, but not as perfect as my mom's.

A few years ago, our family gathered at our ancestral home in Kerala, India, for the wedding of my nephew. Frail yet feisty at 85, Mom decided to pass the baton to me. "I know you make *laddu* in America, now you can make it here," she said.

My mother had asked me to make her signature dish—under her supervision, of course; I felt honored, scared, and excited all at the same time.

My mom was uncompromising in kitchen matters. She supervised a spacious kitchen with several wood burning stoves, racks filled with copper, bronze, and soapstone pots, and a flock of servants who carried out her every instruction.

"Mom, are you sure you want to make *laddu* in *ammuyi's* (grandmother's) kitchen?" my son asked hesitantly. The sentiment was eloquently echoed by the rest of the family. They were wondering how I would cook with wood burning stoves, bronze cookware, no thermometers to gauge temperatures, and no range knobs to adjust heat.

Mom and I started making *laddu* when everyone was taking siesta after lunch. We had the kitchen all to ourselves. As I fed a few tamarind logs into the stove, a worry flashed through my mind–"How am I going to control temperature?"

Mom asked me to pour ghee into a large *uruli* (wide-mouthed bronze pan) and place it on the stove. While the ghee was heating, I prepared *besan* batter to perfect consistency, and started on the sugar syrup on another stove.

"Don't forget to clean the sugar, this is not your clean American sugar," Mom said as she handed me a cup of milk. As I poured milk into the bubbling syrup, dirt rose up instantly; she told me to skim it off. I added the *laddu* coloring to the syrup as Mom pulled up a chair. As the syrup began to thicken, she told me to take a ladleful and drizzle it back into the pan. As it fell, it spun a long thread, like a spider's web.

"It is ready now," Mom said. "Remove the logs from the stove. The charcoal is enough to keep it warm."

By now the ghee in the *uruli* was getting hot; when would it be hot enough to fry the batter?

"Hold your palm just above the ghee," Mom said as though she were reading my thoughts. It was pretty hot and I pulled my hand away instantly.

"Now it is ready," Mom pronounced. "You can start frying batter." I poured a large cup through the *kannappa* (multi-holed ladle). Tiny beads formed, and seconds later, rose to the surface. I scooped them out with a small *kannappa* and transferred them to the syrup. When all the batter was used up, I removed the pan from the stove and set it aside. In a small skillet, I fried cashew nuts and raisins in ghee and poured the mixture over the *besan* beads. As I started stirring, Mom said "Stir gently, otherwise you are going to break the beads."

She called out for our cook to move the heavy *uruli* to the dining room, where it sat under a whirling ceiling fan for several minutes. As the beads cooled, the family gathered. After half an hour, several of us dipped our palms in warm milk, took handfuls of beads, and shaped them into *laddu*.

Following tradition, a few days before the ceremony, wedding guests dropped by to see the bridal gifts from the groom's family. After viewing the colorful clothes and gold necklaces, they were ushered into the dining room for snacks. After devouring the last piece of *laddu* from her plate, a guest told Mom, "I know where this came from; it is your *laddu*."

Mom did not say a word, just smiled and shook her head. Then she slowly turned and glanced at me with a big smile. That was my graduation!

Laddu

Makes 18 to 20

2 c. sugar
¾ c. water
Few drops orange food coloring
2 c. *besan* (Indian chickpea flour, available at Indian groceries)
6 c. ghee (melted clarified butter) or oil for frying
6 T. additional ghee for garnish

12 cashew nuts, broken into small pieces
1 T. seedless dark raisins

1. In heavy skillet over medium heat, combine sugar, water, and food coloring, and cook until mixture reaches one-string consistency syrup (215°F
   to 220°F on candy thermometer). To test doneness, take spoonful of
   syrup, and pour from about two inches above pot. If it spins a long thread
   as it drips, it is done. Set aside.
2. In large bowl, mix *besan* with enough water to make batter of pouring
   consistency (like pancake batter). In heavy saucepan or wok, over medium
   heat, warm ghee (or oil) to approximately 335°F to 340°F. Pour one cup
   batter at a time through slotted spoon with round holes or, if possible, a
   laddu sieve (large metal plate with round holes and handle) into hot fat so
   batter will form beads. Stir and fry beads until crispy and golden. Remove
   beads *(boondi)* with slotted spoon; transfer directly into syrup, and stir.
   Repeat with remaining batter. If syrup becomes too thick, add few drops
   boiling water, and stir.
3. In small skillet over low heat, cook cashew pieces until lightly browned.
   Then add raisins, and remove from stove. Stir nut and raisin mixture into
   skillet of *boondi,* mix well, and cool until it can be handled. Then shape
   into small balls, and place on serving plate.

RUTH'S HOLIDAY CRANBERRY BREAD

Dayna D. Fernandez Wenzel

Most people who celebrate Christmas have fond childhood memories of the
holiday season, such as the anticipation of St. Nick coming down the chimney,
depositing stacks of presents to be torn into on that special pajama-clad
morning. I, however, think of cranberries.

Every December, our homey little kitchen in Los Angeles would transform
into a magical production line of holiday candy and treats. Except for the
annual homemade birthday cakes or homemade pie for the school carnival,
we did not have sweets. As a sugar-deprived kid, I did not appreciate what
a huge favor my parents were doing me. As a result, I grew up with no sweet
tooth at all! I am sure to this day that I am the only woman on the planet
who doesn't eat chocolate because its sweetness "burns my mouth."

But back to the cranberries.

The highlight of our holiday baking was my late mother's cranberry
bread. We would bake for days. It seemed like hundreds of loaves were
produced, although I am sure it was more like a dozen. After cooling, we

would carefully wrap each in plastic, followed by festive gift paper, finished with a pretty bow. Most of these precious loaves were given only to our closest friends and family, and maybe a favorite teacher. We savored the few that were rationed for our family.

The recipients always had the same reaction–"Love it! Very unusual! May I have the recipe please?" The question was politely deflected or ignored. No recipe was ever provided.

Once I grew up and moved away, I always looked forward to coming home for the holidays. I had only one menu request–cranberry bread. It didn't matter what else was going to be served, who cared? Just have that bread ready, please. And a couple of loaves to bring home on the plane.

Cranberry handling is not as easy as it might sound. It involves three steps: careful washing by hand, followed by careful de-stemming by hand (although Ocean Spray does a pretty good job), and finally, cutting each cranberry three times to produce four equal slices. According to my mother, they must be sliced "widthwise, not lengthwise," to ensure optimal "texture" in the final product. When you have sliced enough cranberries, you will realize that they really are slightly longer than wider.

As an adult, I tried shortcuts such as using a food processor or various slicing/dicing machines. They all failed. The bread turned out lumpy or soggy. Only careful hand slicing resulted in the right texture and taste.

And forget about any of those fancy granite countertops that don't stain or scratch. My mother's bread board had a permanent red spot in the middle from the annual slicing. I thought my red fingers were quite festive too, especially since I was too young to wear nail polish.

Once they were sliced, my mother would carefully measure, and immediately add the precious berries as the last ingredient in the secret family recipe. As the loaves baked, the smell was mouthwatering, prompting me to sneak a few tart berries. No, they didn't taste half as good as the bread smelled, but kids like to sneak things behind their mother's back. My brother Nate had the better job as he was usually in charge of nut chopping. Sneaking a walnut is a vast improvement over a raw cranberry.

As an adult, for several years I lived in France, where I began to appreciate that cranberries were indeed a peculiar American berry. Not only did their name not translate into French, they were also not available in local markets. *Mon dieu*! Every berry from the world was displayed at the outdoor market, but not my precious cranberry. Luckily, other Yankees from across the pond were equally starved for their various vittles and someone opened a small shop featuring American packaged goods such as peanut butter and macaroni and cheese. For the price of a fine bottle of wine, I happily procured my bags of Ocean Spray berries and proceeded to make my bread every holiday season.

I still faithfully make cranberry bread each Christmas, playing the role of my mother as I load up my brother with several to take home, and save most for my own consumption. And yes, I too guard the recipe. Even my brother Nate had to repeatedly ask me for it when he wanted to make the bread one holiday season. His guilt trip of reminding me that he was "co-owner" worked. . . and I provided a copy. My dear mother would be proud to know that my brother and I did learn something in her kitchen, and that we honor her memory with her special bread every year.

I even became so fascinated with this versatile little berry that I have collected a number of offbeat recipes over the years that feature cranberries as a key ingredient. Cranberry soup, anyone?

I'm not sure what my mother would say about her secret recipe being published. I hope she is smiling from heaven and gently saying, "Remind them to be careful–don't cut your fingers as you slice your berries."

Cranberry Bread

Makes one medium loaf

2 c. sifted enriched white flour
1 c. sugar
1 ½ t. double-acting baking powder
½ t. baking soda
1 t. salt
2 T. melted shortening or butter
2 T. boiling water
1 egg, well beaten
½ c. finely chopped walnuts
1 ½ c. fresh cranberries, sliced widthwise into fourths
1 orange, rind grated and fruit juiced (juice should measure about ¾ cup)

1. Into medium bowl, sift together flour, sugar, baking powder, baking soda, and salt.
2. In separate medium bowl, combine orange juice, rind, melted butter, and boiling water.
3. Add well-beaten egg.
4. Stir liquid ingredients into dry only until dry ingredients are dampened.
5. Fold in nuts and cranberries.
6. Pour into medium-sized, greased loaf pan.

7. Push batter up into corners, leaving center slightly hollow.
8. Let stand 20 minutes.
9. Meanwhile, preheat oven to 350°F.
10. Bake loaf 50 to 60 minutes.
11. Remove from oven and allow to cool. Then remove from loaf pan and wrap for gift or eat yourself!

RUM CAKE

Maria G. Steinberg

My friend Janie's rum cake spawned a literal mini cottage industry in my hometown of Manila. The cottage is my sister's home where she, her daughters, and house help make rum cakes ordered by many paying friends, acquaintances, and strangers. The recipe has come a long way from Janie's table.

I met Janie when we moved to the United States at the end of my husband's five-year assignment in Hong Kong. Janie is the wife of my husband's best friend. Moving to Connecticut was a monumental change for me, bigger than my move from Manila—where I was born and raised—to Hong Kong where I started married life. I was filled with uncertainty and trepidation at the thought of leaving familiar and much-loved territory and going so far away from my family in the Philippines.

But Janie made sure I felt instantly at home. She was loving and nurturing, the latter manifested mostly in her thoughtful planning and execution of wonderful home-cooked meals for us. During those first few years, we were frequently invited over for meals in Larchmont, New York. I always looked forward to those get-togethers.

I don't exactly remember when she started serving us her rum cake. All I know is that it became a fixture in our brunches and dinners at their home. I truly fell in love with that cake–a tall and handsome Bundt cake, shimmering golden brown on the outside, and radiant sunny yellow on the inside. Janie would often times dust the whole cake with confectioners' sugar, and once in a while she served it drizzled with homemade raspberry sauce. The cake was soft and moist, the bold hint of rum a perfect complement to its sweetness.

When I finally learned to make Janie's rum cake, mine always seemed to suffer by comparison to hers. Somehow, Janie's cakes always seemed taller (even though we used the same-sized pans), moister, and more delectable. My rum cake suffered from an inferiority complex (or maybe I did), and I never served it when Janie was around—not just because hers looked and tasted better, but because this was her signature cake. I would be crossing an inviolable line if I made it and served it to the creator.

What was so special about Janie's cake? It may have had a lot to do with the fact that it is so simple to make, an idiot-proof recipe that uses yellow cake mix as a base. Add eggs, oil, vanilla pudding, and rum to mix, then glaze with a mixture of sugar, butter, and more rum. Only much later on would I admit that what could have added to its great appeal for me was probably my lack of sophistication about food. Gorgeous Bundt cakes were a culinary marvel to me, not having baked much at all growing up. And never mind that it came from a cake mix.

But years later, as my knowledge about food and baking grew and my interest turned from making rum cakes from mixes all the way to tarte tatin from scratch, it occurred to me that what made Janie's rum cake really special was the bond it symbolized between us. This was her way of saying she liked me–the cake was her perpetual friendship offering. Some people give rings to symbolize bonds, but I got beautiful, round, fluted cakes instead. It delighted Janie to see how much I enjoyed her cake. By making it almost every time we saw each other, she reinforced not only her love for baking but her acceptance of me. I felt flattered and comforted. Likewise, she was flattered because I never failed to comment on how delicious it was. It was a symbiotic exchange that went far deeper than the perfect slices she served. Most important, it meant the world to me to have Janie's friendship. She was after all, the best friend of my husband's late wife.

Despite the fact that I felt Janie made the better version, I enjoyed baking this rum cake because I would always get lots of compliments. One thing I did was *Filipinize* the cake by using dark Philippine rum. I always felt good at the thought of adding a touch of home to this all-American recipe. I introduced the cake to my family during visits home, and as expected, they loved it too. My sister started making it for her brood, and then started bringing it to work while her daughters started bringing it to school. One bite led to another and before long, she was in the rum cake business.

My sister eventually made changes to the recipe. She began baking the cakes in loaf pans because, as she explained, it was easier to make and yielded more cakes, making it less costly—important when you're running a business. A more recent innovation is her substitution of margarine for butter in the glaze (okay, I am a little ashamed to say this being a stickler for quality when it comes to ingredients). My sister claims it is just as good.

And so it goes that the original recipe has been altered a bit here and bit there–in shape, size, and even ingredients. With all the cakes and tarts on my list that I still long to make, Janie's cake has not been top of mind for some time now. We also don't see much of each other now that she and her husband have moved to Maryland. But what remains is my enduring fondness for the rum cake–she still makes when we visit—and the special friendship that Janie and I have maintained even to this day.

Janie's Rum Cake

Serves 12

Cake

1 yellow cake mix
4 lg. eggs
1 pkg. instant vanilla pudding mix
½ c. water
½ c. cooking oil
½ c. rum

1. Preheat oven to 325°F.
2. Grease and flour 10-cup Bundt pan.
3. Using electric mixer at medium speed, combine and beat all ingredients for about three minutes.
4. Pour batter into pan.
5. Bake cake for one hour. Cool on wire rack for 20 minutes, then unmold on serving platter, using warm damp dish towel on mold for few seconds to help ease out cake.

Glaze

½ stick unsalted butter
⅛ c. water
½ c. sugar
¼ c. rum

1. Using wooden skewer, poke holes all around cake.
2. In small sauce pan, melt butter.
3. Stir in water and sugar. Boil five minutes, stirring constantly.
4. Remove from heat. Stir in rum and brush mixture on cake.
5. Allow glaze to soak into cake and serve warm or at room temperature.

A SPOONFUL OF INDIA

Liz Tarpy

I didn't learn how to cook from my mother. That's a blessing. Otherwise, I'd be making "stir-boils" with limp vegetables and tasteless chunks of stringy chicken.

I didn't learn how to cook from my grandmother either. And that's a shame. She lavished the table with platters of fresh, simple food: beefsteak tomato salad, corn with salt and butter, juicy burgers, angel food cake. Though she had a better understanding of food and pleasure, Grandma was utilitarian; meals were something you provided without much fuss.

I did learn to cook during college when I got a summer job as a prep cook in Sebasco, Maine. I found I actually liked cooking, even if I was just okay at it. I fell somewhere between my mother and grandmother–I enjoyed putting flavors together, but I was cautious.

By the time I met Anu, something in me was yearning for a deeper connection to food. Anu was first to show me that hard work behind a meal is compensated by the gratification you get when others enjoy it.

My introduction to Anu was in the kitchen of a lodge on the shore of Lake Woodbury, an hour north of Portland, Maine, where I had become an occasional private chef. Anu was a regular guest of Deb and Steve, the owners of the lodge. I was hired to cook their meals when they invited friends from Boston for long weekends. Over the years, Anu was persuaded to share her southern Indian cuisine.

"What is this?" I asked Anu as I lowered my face over a bubbling pot. She ladled out a bowl of soup flecked with green and ushered me to the table. "*Rasam.* Here, try," she invited, smiling.

It was the spiciest soup that ever touched my lips. Each spoonful of thick orange liquid delivered layers of flavor that nourished, healed, and restored. I savored earthy lentils, sweet tomatoes, pungent garlic, and sharp ginger. I took in the delicate aroma of exotic spices like toasted mustard seeds and peppery turmeric.

"Can I eat these things that look like little bay leaves?" I asked.

"Oh yes, they're fresh curry leaves, essential for the special flavor of the *rasam,*" Anu assured me.

I sipped a spoonful, cautiously nibbled on a curry leaf, and was rewarded with a musky citrus flavor. I dove in for more and this time got the fire of chile peppers. I paused to wipe sweat from my forehead. Anu laughed. "I give this to my kids when they don't feel well," she said, "and look at you, your eyes are tearing up!"

As a gift to their hosts that year, Anu and her husband, Anant, brought an authentic tandoor oven. It looked like an oil drum—a pale green metal cylinder about four feet tall and two feet wide with a small door at the bottom where the fire is built. At the top, there was a hole to accommodate long skewers of meat.

Steve helped Anant haul the tandoor from the back of the minivan and plunk it on the driveway. Intrigued by the commotion, Frans and Mathilda, also guests, emerged from their cabin only to be put to work. Anant and Frans built the fire. Mathilda helped Deb thread half chickens, five to a skewer, slick with Anu's deep red tandoori paste.

"Hey guys, is the fire hot enough yet?" Anu yelled from the kitchen. "Everything else is ready, just waiting on you," she teased, carrying a tray of dough balls covered with a dishcloth to the tandoor.

I'd been keeping her company in the kitchen and followed, not wanting to miss a thing. "Let me show you how to make naan," said Anu. She gave me a soft disc of dough and a pink fabric-covered paddle. It was flat on top with some extra fabric gathered underneath for a firm grasp. She placed the dough on the flat side of the puff, and pushed it from the center to the outside, working in a circular motion to cover the entire paddle. Within minutes, she had turned the ball of dough into a six-inch round. "You try."

Holding the puff in my left hand, I patted out the dough as she showed me. "Now, stick your hand into the hole at the top of the tandoor. Then using the paddle, smear the dough on the inside wall so it hangs like a bat in a cave."

Gingerly, I stuck my arm into the hot tandoor with a less-than-perfectly formed naan on my puff. The whoosh of heat took me by surprise; as I jerked my hand back, the silky dough plopped into the fire.

Everyone took a turn, but I outlasted them all, determined to master this skill. It didn't matter to me that by the time I had retrieved a dozen successful naan from the oven, at least the same number had plopped to the bottom. I was in love with the direct connection to the food.

"Dinner!" Anu shouted through the screen door. We headed to the dining room. The long table was cluttered with platters and bowls, giving off seductive smells. Silently, in awe of the feast, we moved along, heaping our plates with fluffy rice–flavored with whole cardamom pods, cubed potatoes tossed with cauliflower and laced with spicy yogurt sauce, and of course, the *rasam*. The naan that I'd worked so hard to make were steaming hot and chewily satisfying. One side was crisp from the hot stone, the other soft and smoky. "You did well," Anu winked at me.

The next day, I persuaded Anu to make her *rasam* again and share her recipe with me. I noted all her techniques, including her method of grinding the ginger into the garlic with the flat of a knife to form a smooth paste. While she dry-roasted chiles and seeds for the *rasam* powder, she told me about growing up in southern India.

By now, the mustard and cumin seeds in the saucepan were popping. Anu sprinkled some *asafoetida*, a pungent plant resin used as a flavoring, into the pan and immediately my nose filled with an acrid sting. She then added handfuls of diced tomatoes, a few fresh curry leaves, and cooked yellow lentils. "We'll let that simmer until it all breaks down."

When the soup reached velvety consistency, Anu scattered chopped cilantro over the top and paused. "I remember my grandmother cooking for me in her tiny, dark kitchen in Hyderabad when I was young. She wore lots of bangles on her wrists. When she tossed the cilantro in at the end, I heard the jingling and knew the *rasam* was ready to eat!"

I no longer spend weekends at Lake Woodbury. But I still make *rasam*. I may not have my grandmother's recipe for angel food cake, but I have this.

Anu's *Rasam*

Serves 6 to 8

1 c. split yellow lentils (*toovar dal*)
2 T. ghee (melted clarified butter)
1 t. mustard seed
1 t. cumin seed
1 t. *asafoetida* powder
1 t. turmeric
Handful fresh curry leaves
2-inch piece ginger, peeled and ground into paste
2 garlic cloves, ground into paste
2 green chiles, split lengthwise
3 tomatoes, chopped
1 t. *rasam* powder (available at specialty or Indian markets)
1 c. cold water
1 bunch fresh cilantro, coarsely chopped
Salt
Juice of 1 lime

1. Cover lentils with water, and in small saucepan over medium heat, cook until soft, adding more water as necessary. Reserve.

2. In large saucepan over very low heat, slowly heat ghee past frothy stage, until translucent. Brown mustard and cumin seeds in ghee until they pop. Add *asafoetida*, turmeric, curry leaves, ginger, garlic, chiles, and tomatoes.
3. Dissolve *rasam* powder in cold water and stir into tomato mixture. Cook over low heat until tomatoes break down. Add reserved cooked lentils and liquid, if any. Continue until lentils soften and lose shape, about 20 minutes.
4. Add cilantro, salt to taste, and lime juice. Swirl and serve.

THE DAY I BECAME THE TYPICAL JEWISH MOTHER

Liora Gvion

"Never follow a recipe," my mom used to say. "They are only meant to give you a general idea."

She was a biochemist and, later on in life, a librarian. Her two professions required precision, accuracy, and yet, when she cooked, she experimented, explored, and mostly improvised. As her dedicated disciple, I, too, thought recipes were never to be taken seriously. Quantities and cooking procedures were nothing but recommendations. Consequently, I could rarely reproduce a successful dish because I never bothered to write anything down.

The Passover seder of spring 1993 almost made me lose faith in my manner of cooking. It has also turned me, according to my children, into the best chicken soup and matzo ball maker on Earth.

My father had passed away only a couple of months earlier. I had a new job and a new baby, and Mom could not bring herself to host the seder. No doubt, I suffered from temporary insanity when I said I would hold the holiday event at my house and invite both of our extended families.

"How are you going to handle all the cooking?" my mother asked.

Well, I didn't intend to. I was going to assign each guest a culinary mission, and try not to worry too much about not having enough forks, knives, and spoons, space, furniture, and plates.

Two days before, it occurred to me that my mom would expect chicken soup with matzo balls, a tasteless dish I never understood why people liked. "Everybody loves chicken soup," she insisted. "And no one can travel with a pot on their lap. We'll just have to make it ourselves."

The thought of her in my messy kitchen while I was moving around living room furniture to seat 25 people was so scary that I decided it was time I made it myself. On that day, I took her basic culinary instruction: "Well, you'll figure it out as you go along" perhaps a little too far.

I looked at the ingredient list, consulted a Jewish cookbook, and panicked. It made no sense to me that these items all cooked together would end up as something edible. I had no choice but to improvise. Don't get me wrong. I cooked the chicken in the pot, but added sweet potatoes, leeks, parsnips, kohlrabi, carrots, parsley, celery root, broccoli, cauliflower, and even a few shitake mushrooms, all cut julienne, of course. Instead of throwing out the chicken after boiling as is common practice, I deboned it, sliced the meat into small pieces and added them to the soup.

The seasoning required more decisions. Although I was extremely generous with fresh ginger, garlic, peppercorns, thyme, and sage, there was something missing. A few spoonfuls of miso and the better part of a bottle of soy sauce came to my rescue.

My mom's recipe for matzo balls reminded me of instructions for making cement, which I knew was dangerous to one's health. So, after mixing the matzo meal with eggs, I traded the schmaltz for olive oil and added huge quantities of every fresh herb I had in my kitchen: parsley, coriander, lemon grass, thyme, sage, and even arugula.

An hour before guests arrived, my oldest daughter and I rolled matzo balls, poking into each either a nut or spoonful of chopped liver, and left them simmering in the soup.

The living room furniture was stored on the balcony, our neighbors loaned us chairs and tables, and the fortune we spent on flowers, beautiful paper plates, tablecloths, cups, eating utensils, and napkins created a stunning table. We were all ready for our family.

As my kitchen filled with other people's containers of more food than we could eat, I decided it was time to enjoy this seder, a holiday I have never ever liked. With some tense family dynamics, a meaningless text, and guests who simply want to eat and get it over, I doubted I could produce an enjoyable evening.

It took two people to carry my huge pot of soup to the table. I served generous portions of what turned out to be a black clear broth soup with thin slices of vegetables, and funny green balls, which I insisted were matzo balls. The diners looked suspicious. For what seemed like an eternity, they neither ate nor said a word. It might have been the intriguing smell, their good manners, or the fear that I might suggest ordering a pizza that induced them to try it. I will never forget their reaction.

"What did you do to the soup?" was the first question, soon followed by "It's amazing; the matzo balls are light and melting in my mouth." On and on they went until my daughter concluded that I had finally become the typical Jewish mother who prepares the best matzo balls on Earth. The guests tried to figure out the ingredients, asking for seconds, and in no time, not a drop of soup was left.

It was then that my mom asked, "You didn't add soy sauce did you? You know it's not kosher for Passover."

I told her I did not. "Thou shall not lie" is not one of the Ten Commandments. If it were, I would still violate it, giving greater allegiance to "Honor thy father and mother."

My mother and I never mentioned my chicken soup again from that day until she passed away in spring 2005, and I have been preparing my version for Passover seder ever since.

Postmodern Chicken Soup

Servings: Depends on appetite

1 chicken
1 celery root
1 parsnip
1 kohlrabi
2 parsley roots
2 lg. carrots
2 to 4 celery stalks
1 sweet potato
1 onion, medium
Shitake mushrooms, reconstituted in water
1 leek
1 head garlic, separated into cloves and peeled
Any other vegetables you fancy
Miso
Fresh ginger
Soy sauce

1. Julienne all vegetables and put in big pot with chicken. Add water, enough to cover by two inches.
2. Bring to boil (skimming off scum as it collects) and simmer until chicken is tender and vegetables are done but not mushy. Turn off burner.
3. When cool enough, remove chicken, cut off skin, and debone. Cut meat in pieces of various sizes and add to soup.
4. Season with salt, pepper, fresh ginger, a few spoonfuls of miso, thyme, sage (fresh is better but dried will do), and as much soy sauce as it takes to make it tasty.
5. Bring back to boil and simmer until vegetables are tender but not mushy.

Herbal Matzo Balls

2 c. matzo meal
2 c. boiling water
3 eggs
4 to 5 T. olive oil
Parsley
Coriander
Sage
Thyme
Arugula
Salt
Pepper
Nutmeg
Nuts
Store-bought chopped chicken livers

1. Chop all herbs. In medium bowl, mix matzo meal, boiling water, eggs, olive oil, and herbs.
2. Season with salt, pepper, and nutmeg.
3. Cover and place in refrigerator for hour or more.
4. With wet hands, roll into balls; push thumb into each and fill with nuts, chopped chicken liver, or anything that comes into your creative mind.
5. Bring soup to boil, add matzo balls and let potage simmer until balls are slightly firmed.
6. Spoon into bowls and serve.

"NOT YOUR MOTHER'S *PIZZELLES*:" MAKING NEW FOOD TRADITIONS

Lynn Marie Houston

Three days after Yuri Gorski died, I devoted a weekend to cooking food for his 99-year-old Polish mother, a woman I had never met. I had only encountered her son once, just a few weeks before the aneurysm. He played in a band with an Iranian friend of mine whom I had just started dating. It was this friend who called to tell me the sad news: Yuri, who lived with his elderly mother, and who my friend suspected was his mother's caregiver, had died in his sleep after receiving a blow on the head earlier that week. My friend asked what we could do for Yuri's mom.

My friend knew I was part Polish and that traditional Polish dishes were a semi-regular presence on our dinner table while I was growing up.

Then, he suggested more than asked, "Maybe you could make her something since you're Polish-American."

I agreed to do it.

One of the only traditional dishes I had ever made was *halupki* (or *galumpki*), a Polish version of stuffed cabbage. I could make a large crock-pot full and freeze portions. It would make hearty meals for the old woman, but she would need something sweet for dessert. One of the only traditional desserts my mother's family makes are crescent-shaped, sour cream dough cookies called *kolachi* (or *kolache*).

Since I was pressed for time, I didn't call my mother for our family recipe; I looked online, followed the instructions to the letter, and the cookies came out quite tasty, but I was left feeling a little unsatisfied; they didn't quite match what I remembered of my mother's *kolachi*.

On Sunday night, I attended Yuri's memorial at a Mexican restaurant (the favorite practice spot of the band in which he had been the lead guitarist) where his family members congregated to remember him and listen to the band's music. I handed over bag after bag of hot food to Yuri's unsuspecting kids to take to their grandmother, a Polish sister-in-spirit whom I had thought about continuously during those two days of cooking but whom I would never meet. She hadn't felt well enough to make the drive from where she lived in the mountains.

About a month later when I went home for Christmas, my mother asked what kind of cookies I wanted to help her make. I quickly said the family traditional recipe for *kolachi*. I was eager to try them to see how they would be different from the Internet recipe. Although the dough was about the same, the Internet *kolachi* had apricot filling rather than traditional nut filling. When it came time to assemble the crescents, my mother didn't seem to have a plan. Had she forgotten how this was done or had there never been a prescribed way? She seemed to make it up as she went along. We split a hot one from the first batch.

"Yep," she concluded, "That's the way they're supposed to taste."

I tasted mine. The dough seemed less flaky and the filling less flavorful compared to the Internet version. When I tried to explain this to her, she became offended. I was disappointed that the "authentic" recipe was nowhere near as good. It left me feeling that any connection to my Polish ancestry wasn't worth trying to maintain. When I returned home from visiting my parents, my Iranian friend listened to me struggle with my identity as a Polish-American.

What did it mean to my identity as a descendant of immigrants to feel that I had found a better tasting cultural product from the Internet than from my own family?

A few months later, I received a package from my mother. It was the *pizzelle* maker that her older sister had passed on to her. The device looks like a waffle griddle; on it you make the crispy, thin, Italian cookies known as *pizzelles*. I remember growing into a taste for the bitter, real anise flavoring used by my grandmother. My mother included a note: "*Pizzelles* are not Polish but your aunts and grandmother make them every Christmas. I'm not a big fan. I want you to have the machine. Maybe you can find a good recipe on the Internet. It doesn't matter where you get it, as long as you make the food with love and share it with someone special."

My mother's gift made me think that I needed to reconsider my ideas about cultural heritage. While I was far from my Polish roots, it didn't mean that my family hadn't created its own meaningful traditions. I realized that it might be better if I didn't try to reconnect to my "lost culture," but developed new traditions that would represent the multifaceted, global person I had become.

The trajectory from Yuri's death to my mother's note spoke to me about issues in defining authenticity, identity, and tradition. From this, I created a new *pizzelle* recipe, one that would celebrate the special connection I had developed with my Iranian friend who had become at that time the "someone special" with whom I shared most food. Starting with a recipe, I made the *pizelles* my own, replacing my grandmother's anise with rosewater, a traditional Persian flavoring. They turned out fine, as have I. Beyond a delicious recipe for cookies, I have discovered one for creating traditions that offers an empowered sense of self. When we honor a multiplicity of cultural traditions, and reach out in kindness to those we care about, we are fertilizing our cultural roots so that they grow and change, adapting rather than recreating or disowning them.

Rosewater *Pizzelles*

Makes about 75

½ c. unsalted butter, melted
1 c. sugar
1 t. vanilla extract
2 t. rosewater
3 eggs, lightly beaten
2 t. baking powder
1 ¾ c. all-purpose flour

1. Using electric mixer on low speed, cream butter and sugar. Add vanilla and rosewater. Whisk in eggs one at a time with wire whisk.

2. In medium bowl, mix flour and baking powder together and add to mixture in mixer bowl. Set aside for 15 minutes.
3. Drop dough by rounded teaspoonfuls onto both sides of *pizzelle* griddle. Bake until lightly browned (about one minute). Cool and sprinkle with powdered sugar.

Once we come into our own, we truly know who we are. We continue to remember where we've been and honor that as well. We now are the transmitters of wisdom and tellers of tales, carrying on the circle and reciting the narratives of the dishes that are our family favorites.

Notes

DEDICATION

1. Stevenson, Robert Louis. "To Auntie," *A Child's Garden of Verses.* London: Wordsworth Editions, Ltd., 1994, p. 132.

CHAPTER 1

1. Bishop, Marion. "Speaking Sisters: Relief Society Cookbooks and Mormon Culture," *Recipes for Reading,* Anne Bower, ed. Amherst: University of Massachusetts Press, 1997, p. 103.

CHAPTER 2

1. Oates, Joyce Carol. *American Appetites.* New York: Harper & Row, 1990, pp. 40–41.

CHAPTER 3

1. Michaels, Anne. *The Winter Vault.* New York: Alfred A. Knopf, 2009, p. 77.

CHAPTER 4

1. Aptheker, Bettina. *Tapestries of Life: Women's Work, Women's Consciousness, and the Meaning of Daily Existence.* Amherst: University of Massachusetts Press, 1989, p. 43.

CHAPTER 5

1. Cunningham, Marion. *Lost Recipes: Meals to Share with Friends and Family.* New York: Alfred A. Knopf, 2003, p. x.

CHAPTER 6

1. Lust, Teresa. *Pass the Polenta.* South Royalton, Vermont: Steerforth Press, 1998, p. 241.

Index

About the Contributors

Meredith E. Abarca is an associate professor at the University of Texas, El Paso, and the author of *Voices in the Kitchen: Views of Food and the World from Working-Class Mexican and Mexican-American Women* (Texas A & M University Press, 2006). Her work has appeared in *Food & Foodways,* edited collections, and encyclopedias. She has lectured in Italy, Spain, Mexico, and South America.

Arlene Voski Avakian is a professor and the director of women's studies at the University of Massachusetts, Amherst. She is the editor of *Through the Kitchen Window: Women Explore the Intimate Meaning of Food and Cooking* (Beacon Press, 1997), and co-editor of *From Betty Crocker to Feminist Food Studies: Critical Perspectives on Women and Food* (University of Massachusetts Press, 2005).

Ellen Perry Berkeley is a writer living in Shaftsbury, Vermont. Her book *At Grandmother's Table: Women Write about Food, Life, and the Enduring Bond between Grandmothers and Granddaughters* (Fairview, 2000) was hailed as one of the year's top ten cookbooks by the *Los Angeles Times.*

Janet Chrzan holds a PhD in physical/nutritional anthropology from the University of Pennsylvania, where she is a lecturer in the department of anthropology and school of nursing. Her research explores the connections between social activities, nutritional intakes, and mother and child health outcomes in pregnant teens.

Mildred Pierson Davella was born to Swedish immigrants in 1917. She died in 2009 at age 92, and was much loved by her husband, daughters, son, granddaughter and niece, Linda Berzok, for—among many things— her culinary prowess.

Rebecca Libourel Diamond, who has a background in both journalism and library science, has had a varied career combining writing and research. Her passion for cooking developed by observing her home economics-trained mother, grandmother, and aunts perform culinary masterpieces. She is currently writing a book about the history of U.S. cooking schools.

Carol Durst, PhD, has taught at and served in the administration of several New York metropolitan universities in culinary, food studies, hospitality, and tourism programs. She was the first director of the New York Restaurant School, owned a catering business, and wrote *I Knew You Were Coming So I Baked a Cake* (Simon & Schuster, 1997).

Patricia Espinosa-Artiles was born in Camagüey, Cuba, and grew up in Ciego de Avila. She has degrees in agricultural engineering and plant biotechnology. In 2004, she immigrated to the United States. She lives in Tucson, Arizona, and works at a research plant science lab at the University of Arizona.

Anita Gallers was born and raised in the Bronx, New York, and still visits her parents there. Her grandmother, Sadie Gallers, lived most of her 98 years there, too, and was known for her artistry with knitting needles as well as her *rugelach*. Anita teaches young moms at The Care Center in Holyoke, Massachusetts.

Janie Goldenberg is a recent transplant to New Mexico where she works, cooks, paints and writes. She lives with her husband and dog, and some permutation of their five children.

Rebecca Gopoian writes poems, stories, book reviews, articles, and cartoon essays. Her work has appeared in the *New York Times*, *Denver Quarterly*, *Jubilat*, and *Drunken Boat*, among other journals. She lives with her husband, cartoonist David Heatley, and their two children in Jackson Heights, Queens.

Liora Gvion was born in Israel and grew up there and in Belgium, France, and Brazil. She is a sociologist whose areas are the sociology of food and the body. Her work centers on changes in diets caused by immigration, nation-building, and globalization. She is currently studying the culinary practices of migrant-laborers in Israel.

Annie Hauck-Lawson, RD, PhD, is president of the Association for the Study of Food and Society, author of *Gastropolis: Food & New York City* (Columbia University Press, 2008), and an associate professor at Brooklyn College. Her scholarship concerns the "food voice," a term she originated for how foodways serve as channels of communication and expressions of identity.

Lisa Heldke is author of *Exotic Appetites: Ruminations of a Food Adventurer* (Routledge, 2003), and co-editor of two food-related works of philosophy—*Cooking, Eating, Thinking: Transformative Philosophies of Food* (Indiana University Press, 1992), and *The Atkins Diet and Philosophy* (Open Court, 2005). She is a professor of philosophy and holds the Sponberg Chair in Ethics at Gustavus Adolphus College.

Lynn Marie Houston is an assistant professor of literature in the English department at California State University, Chico. She teaches a course on food and literature, as well as other courses in American literature, postcolonial literature, and women's literature.

Sharon Hudgins is a food and travel writer and editor. She is author of *The Other Side of Russia: A Slice of Life in Siberia and the Russian Far East* (Texas A & M University Press, 2004) and *Spanien: Küche, Land und Menschen* [*Spain: The Cuisines, The Land, The People*] (Hadecke, 1991). She is currently the food columnist for *German Life* magazine (USA) and the food editor for European Traveler Web site.

Tijen Inaltong researches food and its rituals in her native country of Turkey and abroad. She has written ten gastronomy books and translated four, taught cooking, and contributed to newspapers, magazines and collective books. She believes it is necessary to record our traditions before they disappear from our lives.

Sharon L. Jansen lives in Steilacoom, Washington. She is the author of several books on medieval and Renaissance women, most recently *Debating Women, Politics, and Power in Early Modern Europe* (Palgrave Macmillan, 2008) and *Anne of France: Lessons for My Daughter* (Boydell & Brewer, 2004).

Kelly Jeske reads, writes, and chases her toddler, Quincy LaTasha, in Portland, Oregon. She has a master's degree in sociology and works on the board of directors for Adoption Mosaic. Her writing appears in the anthology *Who's Your Mama? The Unsung Voices of Women and Mothers* (Soft Skull Press, 2009).

Ellen Kaye is a New York City-based writer who has contributed to the *New York Times*, the *Los Angeles Times*, and *CHOW* Magazine, among others. She is co-author of *The Wine Guy: Everything You Want to Know About Buying & Enjoying Wine From Someone Who Sells It* (William Morrow/HarperCollins 2005).

Annie Lanzillotto is a memoirist, songwriter, poet, and performance-artist, whose first book is forthcoming from the SUNY Albany Press. Publications include "Cosa Mangia Oggi" in *Gastropolis: Food and New York City* (Columbia University Press, 2008) and "Triple Bypass" in *The Milk of Almonds: Italian-American Women Writers on Food and Culture* (Feminist Press, 2000).

Susan J. Leonardi lives, cooks, and eats in Davis, California. A recovering academic, she does free-lance writing, including her community newsletter, "The Covell (Un)Common Rag," and the wine column ("Wineaux") for the Davis *Enterprise*. Her publications include *And Then They Were Nuns: A Novel* (Firebrand Books, 2003), *Dangerous by Degrees* (Rutgers University Press, 1989), and *The Diva's Mouth* (Rutgers University Press, 1996).

Ditte Lokon moved to the U.S. from Bali, Indonesia, in 1981. She loves to travel, and enjoys trying to recreate foods she tastes during her journeys. She lives in Eugene, Oregon.

Lucy M. Long is the author of *Culinary Tourism* (University Press of Kentucky, 2004), *Regional American Food Culture* (Greenwood Press, 2009), and numerous articles on foodways. She has a PhD in folklore, a master's in ethnomusicology, and teaches at Bowling Green State University, Ohio. She also directs the non-profit Center for Food and Culture.

Irene MacCollar, writer and artist, resides in coastal Maine. Her writing credits include publication in the anthology *Poet's Cove* (New Monhegan Press, 2003), a spot in the top ten among more than 2,000 screenplay submissions to actor Kevin Spacey's TriggerStreet.com, and first place in the Louise Wahl Creative Writing Contest for her original poem "Fragments."

Ashley Makar is a poet, student at Yale Divinity School, and contributing co-editor of *Killing the Buddha*, an online religion writing magazine. She is grateful to her Egyptian Aunt Elena, her Alabamian mother, Barbara, and grandmothers Pauline and Mildred, for speaking to her the first poetry of her life.

Marty Martindale has a background in broadcasting, copywriting, and hospitality marketing. She has published in *Gourmet Retailer* and several food reference volumes. In 2001, she founded http://www. FoodSiteoftheDay.com, a weekly review of food Web sites. She received an Addy Broadcasting Award and the 2005 *Cordon d'Or*, crystal globe Web site award.

Renee Marton was a chef for 15 years before becoming a culinary school instructor and food historian. She has published on diverse topics including the story of the grilled cheese sandwich in America and the history of commercial fishing.

Kristen Miglore left her economics career in 2007 to pursue a master's degree in food studies at New York University, and has found herself cooking, writing, and eating her way through New York City ever since. She has written on food for *Saveur, Restaurant Business*, and *The Martha Stewart Show.*

Devon Abbott Mihesuah, a member of the Choctaw Nation of Oklahoma, is the Cora Lee Beers Price teaching professor in international cultural understanding at the University of Kansas. She is the author of many books, most recently, *Recovering Our Ancestors' Gardens: Indigenous Recipes and Guide to Diet and Fitness* (University of Nebraska Press, 2005), and is a recipient of the Special Award of the Jury from the Gourmand World Cookbook Awards.

Kim Morgan Moss is a baker and mother of three. She lives in Charleston, South Carolina, where she writes from her kitchen for "A Yankee in a Southern Kitchen," a food blog.

Traci Marie Nathans-Kelly earned her PhD in 1997, culminating in her dissertation "Burned Sugar Pie: Women's Cultures in the Literature of Food." Publishing variously on women's use of recipes in storytelling, she also loves talking to local historical groups about the potential of community cookbooks as historical documents.

Jashio Pei was born in Chung King, Szechuan, China, and moved to the United States to study art at the Rhode Island School of Art and Design. After working as a graphic artist, she retired and focused her attention on ceramic painting. Having learned to make pot stickers as a young girl, she made them as a treat to relish in America.

Gillian Polack, PhD, is a historian and writer, based in Australia. Over 200 pieces of her writing have been published, from scholarly articles to novels and prize-winning short stories. Recent publications include the novel *Life Through Cellophane* (Eneit Press, 2009) and an anthology *Masques* (co-edited with Scott Hopkins, CSFG Publishing, 2009).

Ammini Ramachandran is the author of *Grains, Greens, and Grated Coconuts* (iUniverse, 2007). Her recipes appear in *The Flavors of Asia* by the Culinary Institute of America (DK Publishing, 2009). She has contributed to *Sacred Waters* (Adams Media, 2005) and *Entertaining from Ancient Rome to the Super Bowl* (Greenwood Press, 2008).

D'Arcy Smylie Randall is a founder of *Borderlands: Texas Poetry Review*. Her recent works appear in *Prairie Schooner* and *Letters to the World: Poems from the Wom-Po LISTSERV* (Red Hen Press, 2008). She holds a PhD from the University of Texas, Austin, where she now teaches writing in the department of chemical engineering.

Rachelle H. Saltzman, folklife coordinator (Iowa Arts Council), writes about foodways and ethnic folklore. She created the Iowa Place-Based Foods Web site, and has written for *Edible Iowa, The Snail,* the *Journal of American Folklore, Anthropological Quarterly, Journal of Folklore Research, New York Folklore, Southern Folklore, Southern Exposure,* and edited collections.

Joy Santlofer, adjunct instructor in the food studies program at New York University, has written for *Gastropolis: Food & New York City* (Columbia University Press, 2010), and *Food, Culture and Society.* She is working on a book about the history of food production in New York to be published by W.W. Norton.

Elena Schwolsky-Fitch is a public health educator in New York City whose writing explores the intersection of her personal and professional life on the frontlines of the AIDS epidemic in the United States and Cuba. Elena received the Barbara Deming/Money for Women Fund award for her memoir in progress.

Tamara Sharp is a graduate student in American culture studies at Bowling Green State University. Her research focuses on foodways, particularly in terms of cultural identity, with interests in race and ethnicity. She is currently working on her thesis on foodways of Appalachian outmigrants.

Amy Cyrex Sins lives in New Orleans and is the author of *Ruby Slippers Cookbook: Life, Culture, Family & Food After Katrina* (Amy Cyrex Sins, 2006). As a cooking enthusiast, she spends every free moment in the kitchen creating meals for friends and family.

Alexandra Springer is a lecturer and PhD candidate at the University of Hawai'i at Manoa. She is currently working on her dissertation using the Slow Food movement as a case study to explore the multifaceted, dynamic relationship between the movement and its local, national, and transnational environment.

Maria G. Steinberg is a marketing manager for a New York City-based specialty food company and a food writer. She has a master's degree in food studies from New York University and is a graduate of Le Cordon Bleu in Paris. Her food articles have appeared in publications including Gamberro Rosso's *Questione di Gusti.*

Sian Supski is a research fellow at Monash University, Victoria, Australia. She was awarded her PhD from Curtin University in 2003. Her research interests include 1950s kitchens in Australia and Australian cookbooks. Her publications include *It Was Another Skin: The Kitchen in 1950s Western Australia,* (Peter Lang, 2007). She thanks Peter Beiharz for his encouragement.

Liz Tarpy is a freelance culinary researcher, writer, recipe editor and tester, and owner of Teaberry Productions. Her writing has been published in *Saveur* and *German Life,* and online at starchefs.com and delish.com.

Betty Teller worked for 20 years as an exhibition developer at the Smithsonian Institution. In 1998, she moved to California as founding exhibitions director of Copia: The American Center for Wine, Food & the Arts. Since 2005, she has pursued a second career as an editor and food writer of a weekly column in the *Napa Register.*

Heather Wearne is a writer and university teacher based in Brisbane, Australia. She has been teaching literature and writing at the Australian University for many years as well as running community writing programs in life writing. Her doctoral research interest was autobiographical writing and the lives of "ordinary" women.

Dayna D. Fernandez Wenzel is a certified project manager in the software industry. She was born, raised, and educated in Los Angeles County, California. She has fond memories of growing up in her mother Ruth's kitchen, while her father, Delbert, and brother, Nate, sampled their creations. Dayna resides in Connecticut with her taste-tester husband, Richard.

Jeanette Williams is a food enthusiast and former restaurateur. She lives in central New Jersey and teaches at Promise Culinary Arts School with a focus on restaurant operations and sustainability. She holds a bachelor of arts from the New School with a focus on creative writing and literature.

AnnaLee Wilson is writing a memoir based on her experiences as owner of Kaeser and Wilson Design, Ltd. in Manhattan. Her short story, "Playing to Win," appeared in *The First Line*, Winter 2005. She has written for the newsletter *Character Matters* and co-hosts the One Page Poetry Circle at the New York Public Library.

About the Editor

Linda Murray Berzok is a food historian and writer, author of "My Mother's Recipes: The Diary of a Swedish-American Mother and Daughter," an essay in *Pilaf, Pozole and Pad Thai: American Women and Ethnic Food* (University of Massachusetts Press, 2001), and *American Indian Food* (Greenwood Press, 2005). She is a member of the Association for the Study of Food and Society and a founding member of *Sabores Sin Fronteras*/Flavors without Borders in Tucson, Arizona. Linda holds a master's degree in food studies from New York University, and is an avid, multicultural cook.